MONEY MIND CRUSH

Fed Up Being Broke And Frustrated? Attract All The Money You Could Ever Want By Discovering The Money Magnet That Lives In Your Head

KEITH EVERETT

CONTENTS

Foreward — v
Introduction — vii
Disclaimer — xi

1. The Power of You — 1
2. My CRAZY Life. Yes, a bit about me.. — 11
3. The Golden Triangle — 16
4. Freedom, The Ultimate High — 30
5. The Magic House — 39
6. The Art of Rich Thinking — 43
7. Just Do It — 54
8. The Weirdness of Lies — 64
9. The Millionaire Business Model — 70
10. Family, Friends and Foes — 80
11. The Art of Making money — 86
12. Self-Doubt - Winning Through It — 90
13. The Enemy Within — 96
14. Niches and Riches — 100
15. Unclutter Your life — 111
16. The Fantasy of Luck — 118

Conclusion — 125
Resources — 127

FOREWARD

I dedicate this book to my parents, Alex and Joan who not only gave me life but gave me the encouragement to be the best I could be.

They never gave up on me, even when I tried to screw my life up in my teenage years.

Thank You Mum and Dad.

INTRODUCTION

I have spent the last 40 years learning how to think, act and become more prosperous. Believe me, it wasn't easy.

I have realised from an early age, that no one in this life is going to make you a better version of yourself. Only you can do that.

I have created multiple businesses in my life, some were spectacular failures and others created multiple six-figure incomes.

This book will teach you how to change your mindset from poor and broke, to being able to produce rich and wealthy thoughts, that transcend into real, tangible RICHES.,

People tend to operate on having two Bank accounts. Their emotional Bank account and their financial Bank account.

The emotional bank account always leads the financial one. How you think, creates what you earn. To earn more, upgrade your thinking.

How much we have in the bank should never decide your self-worth, however people often see the lack of funds in their physical bank account as a poor reflection of their self worth.

Nothing could be further from the truth. You don't become rich and then become a better person. You become a better person, then you can become rich.

You may have read dozens of books on how to become rich, and I bet some were good, but I can guarantee that a lot of them were probably a waste of time.

The reason being, many books are written by people who haven't actually done the things that they write about. This can be very annoying, as a lot of the things that they do write about, don't actually work in practice.

How can someone talk about wealth when they have never experienced it. With this book, I can guarantee you that everything you learn here, are actual tactics and techniques that I've used personally to lift myself out of the poverty trap, and create a great life.

It's far better to try things and fail, than it is to never risk a thing, and always be wondering what might have been.

Let's be honest. Normal life SUCKS!!. It's like a non stop treadmill of work and paying bills, with very little to show for it at the end of the day.

Being broke is downright embarrassing, checking prices all the time and trying to save a bit here and a bit there, especially when your friends are out there driving better cars, having better clothes, houses and holidays.

So how is this book different from the many others out there?.

First of all, this is my personal journey of discovery which took me over 40 yrs to learn and get right. You're getting my 40 years of experience for a few dollars.

I tell everything exactly like it is. I'm not saying anything here that I haven't done myself. Once I discovered the power of the mind, I never looked back.

Life is too short to always be traveling second class.

I wanted First class in everything, and I made sure I got it.

Now it's your turn.

This book is about how I actually developed the wealth mindset at a very early age. In fact it was a shock visit to my deceased grandad's house when I was a kid that actually started the ball rolling.

In this book I will reveal everything. Read it from cover to cover, and over and over again. It is also out on Audible, listen to it over and over again until it becomes a big part of your life. Don't miss a thing. I am going to take you on a magnificent journey of your own self-discovery.

I am going to show you how to peek through the window of your very soul and show you how to alter your state of mind, the mind that is holding you back.

No one wants to stay stuck in life. It's painful and it's also very soul destroying. Let me take you on an exciting journey. A journey to a better life for you and your family.

Discover how to let go of the previous thinking that may be keeping you broke, unsatisfied and broken. Learn how you can develop the system of wealth attraction, that I've been using for years.

Are you ready?

Buckle up and enjoy the ride, here we go.

P.S I have a very special free gift for you at: https://keitheverett.co.uk/special

DISCLAIMER

The content contained within this book may not be reproduced, duplicated or transmitted without direct written permission from the author or the publisher.

Under no circumstances will any blame or legal responsibility be held against the publisher, or author, for any damages, reparation, or monetary loss due to the information contained within this book. Either directly or indirectly. You are responsible for your own choices, actions, and results.

<u>Legal Notice:</u>

This book is copyright protected. This book is only for personal use. You cannot amend, distribute, sell, use, quote or paraphrase any part, or the content within this book, without the consent of the author or publisher.

<u>Disclaimer Notice:</u>

Please note the information contained within this document is for educational and entertainment purposes only. All effort has been executed to present accurate, up to date, and reliable, complete information. No warranties of any kind are declared or implied. Readers acknowledge that the author is not engaging in the rendering of legal, financial, medical or professional advice. The content within this book has been derived from various sources. Please consult a licensed professional before attempting any techniques outlined in this book.

By reading this document, the reader agrees that under no circumstances is the author responsible for any losses, direct or indirect, which are incurred as a result of the use of the information contained within this document, including, but not limited to, — errors, omissions, or inaccuracies.

Copyright Keith Everett 2021 - All rights reserved.

❧ 1 ❧

THE POWER OF YOU

Although we all find it hard to admit..

We are totally responsible for where we are at this point in our lives.

I know that sounds harsh, and you could probably come up with a dozen reasons why things didn't work out for you, but in truth, it's always been about us. We did it to ourselves.

Oh sure. This went wrong, that went wrong, I got married, had kids, got sick, got in trouble with the law. I think we can all come up with a dozen or more reasons why we didn't get Rich.

But, the truth is. It's all our fault. Now, bear with me here.

There's no need to feel guilty. This is not what this book is about. In the end, it was our thoughts, our decisions and our habits (good or bad) that brought us to this point in our lives.

Change always has, and always will begin with you. Yes, there are all kinds of other components to being a success but you are and will always be your biggest asset ,or your biggest liability.

It's up to you to choose which one. asset or liability?.

We all have a choice. Because, the only person in the World who can stop you from being a Success, a Millionaire – (XXXXX) insert whatever you want, is YOU.

Let me explain.

We all have circumstances in life that can hold us back. It may range from not having enough money to having an unsupportive spouse or partner.

There will always be hurdles in your way. This is just how life works. And you'll still have hurdles, even when you become a Millionaire.

The hurdles just get bigger..

So, let's take a little responsibility (I hate that word) for ourselves here and admit, we are responsible for our own life, successes etc, no one else...

The thing is, there are plenty of people who have the same hurdles that we have, but they just don't let it stop them. In order to get where we want to go, we have to step over our disadvantages and just break down that door.

We can't keep playing the blame game..

Maybe you don't play the blame game at all, but many people do, they blame everything and everyone but themselves. If you do, it's not attractive. It is the weapon of the weak, it helps the weak justify their lack of success.

Once we can get over our worst enemy (ourselves), we can literally do anything. We can create our own habits. It is these habits that shape our lives for good or bad.

Our habits have also created how we view ourselves, how we view other people and even how we view the World.

Everyone has their own version of the world, we are all starring in our own movies and our friends, family and acquaintances are either co-stars or extras in our movie.

This means that others will see you as either a co-star or extra too. Bear this in mind.

We are where we are because of who we've become. Everything you have done, your thoughts and your habits along the way, plus the actions you have taken, have led you to where you are today.

Angry people are people who are hurting inside. The truth is, the world is neither a good or a bad place, it is only how we ourselves view it.

The good thing is, we can change ourselves quickly, by the way we think. We are not creatures without intelligence (although some may argue this point), we can always change how we think about things, and how we react to them.

I don't know you personally but in essence, maybe I do. You're probably not a lot unlike me. A person who wants to do better, maybe someone who wants to make an impact in this World. Someone who wants to be heard and recognised for who they really are.

We all want to feel significant.

Most people never give themselves the chance to be great. Their time is taken up with complaining and criticising others. This is not only destructive to people around you but it's also ripping the heart out of you.

I believe we all have a talent. You may not see yours right now, but as you delve deeper into the secrets within this book, you will begin to find yours.

This is the right time and place.

Life should be simple. It should be something you savour, not something you struggle with. Unfortunately for many it's not, life is hard. We have people to please, money to make, bills to pay, opinions to live up to, and all sorts of other stuff buzzing around in our heads, and we also have to try and keep healthy and keep going.

How many times do we try to live up to the good opinion of other people?

Sometimes it can all get a bit much and we just get down, we may even get depressed. I think most of us have felt this way, it's like our life has got out of our control and left us behind at some stage, it can sometimes feel like we've lost our way.

We get stale, we can even lose our mojo. This leads to a period of nothingness, and leads to us spinning our wheels and feeling like we are going nowhere.

I have news for you. This is normal, and most people experience this several times throughout their lives

But all is not lost.

Although having lots of money won't make your life perfect, it will give you more choices in life. It will give you more control. And this is what a lot of people feel that they are lacking in. Control over their own life, control over their own future.. They feel absolutely stuck..

Prepare to get unstuck..

Most people are living their lives at the mercy of others. Many are just one or two pay cheques away from being broke. The loss of a job can have a devastating effect on the family and can also really affect a relationship with your spouse or partner.

But why is it most people don't have enough money?

The answer to this is simple.

They either don't earn enough, or they spend more than they earn. It's a vicious circle. Even people with money can find themselves broke if they keep upgrading their lifestyle way past their income.

We may have a job, we turn up every week and we get paid. Maybe we'll win the lottery (fat chance), We don't think anything serious is going to happen to us (apart from Death).. And even that is a long way off, right?

The truth is, things do happen. Jobs get cut, we lose things, crash cars, need plumbers etc. People get sick. We don't always have the funds on tap to deal with life's emergencies.

So we borrow. And from here, it's a never ending game of trying to play catch up.

We spend countless hours trying to juggle balls. Pay this, pay that, do this, do that. No wonder many of us just want to sit in front of the TV each night and relax with a glass, or two.

Of course, some blame it on bad luck. Although luck does play a small part, around 95% of what happens to us is actually down to us alone, and has nothing to do with luck.

We may think sometimes that our lives are really out of control, but most of our lives can be controlled by ourselves, if only we could change the way in which we think.

Well, you can.

Also, no matter what life throws at us, we tend to attract the things that are in tune with our thoughts. If life is tough, it's usually because we keep trying to opt for an easy life. Life will be hard if we're always looking for the easy life, and life will be easy if we're prepared to go at it hard.

This may not make a lot of sense right now, but it will.

There is a specific way of thinking that people have been taught to think is the right way. It's usually the way we are brought up and taught in school.

1. Get good at passing tests

2. Get a job or career.

Although these are not bad things, people are never really taught the realities of life. What looks good on paper doesn't necessarily work out in the great big world.

Get a job, get a girlfriend/boyfriend, get a house, get married, have kids, live happily ever after, I think you get the idea...

I'm not saying there's anything wrong with this. But people stick to this line throughout their lives and never veer off of it. Call it what you will, we can call it your comfort zone if you like.

The trouble with the comfort zone is it's very restricting. People tend to live in the same local town most of their life, they have one or two holidays a year, they generally keep the same friends and visit the same places.

If you're OK with that, that's fine. But to be a Millionaire, you have to think like one. They think differently to most people, this is obvious as most people never become one.

But most people CAN become one.

If you are prepared to change your thinking and relax your own rules, you can achieve anything. In other words, the comfort zone you currently live in needs to expand.

It is my belief that everyone can get Rich, it's not that people can't do it, it's that most people won't do it because it means stretching their comfort zone in order to do it.

And that's where the problem lies. People don't like to change their current way of doing things in order to create more.

The answer:

Create a NEW normal..

> "If we change the way we look at things, the things we look at change"
>
> — WAYNE DYER

Merge your new routine to fit in with your old routine.

If your new routine is to create more money and to start a business from home, do so whilst still retaining your day job.

No one has to quit their job straight away to start a business. Not unless you have enough money to live on for the next year.

It's always a challenge at the start of any new venture. As I said earlier, there will always be hurdles to overcome. Don't worry about them - just expect them.

If possible, get everyone around you on board. No matter how skeptical they are at the moment, involve those who are willing.

Don't push the family away when you start a new venture, this is a very common mistake, if you do this, they will resent the new venture (and you).

Make your friends and/or family part of the equation. Your life will never be the same again, so get those around you to embrace it and get used to it.

If you can't get people on your side at first, don't worry too much, when people see your success first hand, they will usually get on board with it.

Most people need to see it working before they believe it. As an Entrepreneur you will take a different approach. You will believe it before you see it.

Visualise what you want as if you already have it.

First, see it happening in your mind's eye. Get a feel for what it will be like once you've achieved it. Some may call this daydreaming, but in order to achieve your dream you will need to start living it before you actually have it in your grasp.

You are now on your way to thinking differently.

Instead of seeing a problem with every opportunity, start to see an opportunity in every problem.

The first real key to change is to want to change. Admit that you have made mistakes in the past (as we all have) and make it your number one goal to change your habits NOW.

We all have the ability to learn. But it doesn't stop when we leave school or college. Life should be about continuous learning. You can't learn everything about everything, but you can learn a lot more than you already know about something.

And now is the exact time to start learning how to become a Millionaire.

A Million is just a very big number that can be broken down into a series of smaller numbers. You don't have to make the million today, but you can get started today.

Let me give you an example.

If you look at a professional photographer, my guess is that not many of them are millionaires, I'm sure there are some out there, but just because you are a photographer and you do an occasional wedding at the weekends, it doesn't mean that you can't become a millionaire.

You just have to think outside the box.

One million pounds (or dollars) is 2739 per day if you try to do this over 1 year. It's a mere 547 per day if you take five years.

A photographer can either remain just a photographer or if he/she flips that switch in his/her head they can DECIDE to be a millionaire photographer instead..

Here's how.

1 wedding per weekend is done at a cost of £400 (or dollars) giving approx. £20,000 Per year or £100,000 per 5 yrs.

3 x in-house child portrait sessions per week at £100 a time = £300 per week or £15,000 per year (£75,000 over 5 yrs)

Professional in-house photography courses sold at £1000 each (time taken 3 days) 2 sold per month = £24,000 per year or £120,000 over 5yrs.

Personalised photo T shirts and mugs sold online, and through Amazon & eBay £500 profit per week, or £25,000 per year, or £125,000 over 5yrs.

OK, so that's a Whopping £420,000 over 5 yrs and we are just getting going. I could carry on quite easily until we are at the million mark and beyond.

YOU can do this with any business. You just have to change your thinking and think bigger. If you always think a Million is impossible, then it is. This is where you need to view things with a new perspective.

A million pounds (dollars or whatever) is just a big number that you keep breaking down until it's manageable.

Some of my colleagues online are making upwards of $20,000 a month, all through learning to be better at what they do. They all started out small and grew as their thinking grew. They are ordinary people with families and mortgages, bills and all that other stuff.

They choose to be less ordinary.

If they can do it, so can you.

STOP settling for less. We were all born to make life the best we can make it. Trust me when I say, having a million will make it run a whole lot better.

I've been in business over 40 yers now, made and lost several fortunes, I've made just about every mistake in the book, so you can now benefit from my mistakes.

NEXT: My Back Story - No, I'm not going to give you a load of boring stuff about me, just the important bits..

By the way, once you've read the book why not join my free Private Facebook group. It's called Inspired To Make Money

OK, so i'm being a bit over generous now. I have a very nice free gift waiting for you at https://keitheverett.co.uk/special

I digress. On to the next chapter.

❧ 2 ❧
MY CRAZY LIFE. YES, A BIT ABOUT ME..

My Journey.

I've loved making money and helping people ever since I was a kid in short trousers. Yes, kids of my generation wore hideous short trousers.

Much to the annoyance of my folks, I regularly sold off my toys in garage sales when I was a kid.

A friend of mine, Ronald Grace, and I often held raffles for Easter eggs & chocolates, and just about nailed it in my neighbourhood as the "Go to guys" for stuff.

We were "killing it", You name it, we had it, slightly used toys, comics, books and just about anything else we could get our hands on.

I was convinced in those days that I could sell anything, even the kitchen sink, although I don't think my Mum would have been very happy with that idea.

This was all before I was 12.

At 13, I was a bus nut (someone who loves buses) and created a newsletter for people who were as nutty about buses as me. This was a monthly newsletter that I sold on subscription.

My dad had a fit one day when a man knocked on our front door wanting to meet the editor of the newsletter. I was only a kid, but even then, I was a kid who knew that I was going places.

Even though I wasn't very confident in other areas (chasing girls, sports etc), because at school I was quite short, however, I channeled that initial lack of confidence into thinking bigger. I felt very confident at selling and making money.

Strange as it may seem, making money your own way can make you feel more confident.

My Mum and Dad were very good sports, they let me grow up slowly and develop my entrepreneurial mind. They never pushed me toward any type of trade.

After spending the latter part of my teens generally being a nuisance and spending time with street gangs and other such undesirables, I finally decided I wanted to make it BIG in the world of business.

My big break came when I sailed out of my teens and after surviving many run-ins with the police, I entered my twenties.

I joined a bookmaking chain (Turf Accountants - William Hill) at age 20, and I learnt about sports, and how to make money from them.

People bet, most are mugs, end of story.

I became a very successful Bookmaker myself at age 21, I bought a small bookmakers in Camberley, Surrey, England using my meagre savings plus a hefty loan.

I ran this for a few months taking bets and luckily not paying out too much back to punters. A large bookmaking chain took a shine to the shop, made me an offer, and I sold it to them for a massive profit. Incredibly, after just a few months of running the business and selling it, I had made enough profit from this to pay cash for a house.

The feeling was Awesome...

BOOM! This just fuelled my love of business.

Always stay enthusiastic. If you can't be enthusiastic about a venture longer than five minutes, don't do it.

You need your enthusiasm to get you over the speed bumps during hard times.

One of the things I realised along the way was, that instead of ducking and diving all the time, going from one business to another, why not create a proper business and then once it's profitable, add other related streams of income to it?, then you can either keep it or sell it as a going concern for as much money as you can.

Business is all about creating value for people.

Once I had sold my Betting business for a profit, I could have flipped the money into another Betting business in another town...

Rinse and repeat. This is how you make money, build assets, make profits then sell those assets for as much as you can.

Unfortunately I was a bit naive at that age, I was young, and I spent all the profit from the betting business on good living, chasing girls and booze. The rest, I just wasted.

However, lessons learned.

I did pay the initial loan back to the bank on time though.

Once you do this, the banks will love you, so next time you need money to buy a business, it will be a lot easier.

Create a good relationship with your bank.

I have also owned a Driving School, an Ice Cream business (those annoying vans that drive around streets) I've had an eBay business and several online businesses.

Why am I telling you all this?

I'm not telling you all this to brag, I'm telling you this because I truly believe anyone can make money, and live a great life. I was only educated at a comprehensive school, nothing fancy, I got a basic education, left early, at age sixteen, and I didn't look back.

Education is fine, but education of life is a whole lot better.

People often complain that life is hard, and to be truthful, it is without much money.

However, we are our own worst enemy at times. We tend to put other things in the way of our own success. We want more, but also we want our lives to remain undisturbed.

A business is like taking on another partner, your spouse is one partner, your business is another – you have to maintain both relationships and juggle them both.

Don't go into a business unless you are prepared for upsets, problems and a large chunk of your social life disappearing for a while. Also don't start a business you're not suited to.

People do it all the time. And then they quit in a few months.

Choose a business that you can see yourself doing a year, even five years or more down the line, unless of course you're going to flip it (sell it). Even so, choose a business you like.

If you love to write, create books, Kindle books, audiobooks, and sell them on Amazon. If you love working out and you fancy yourself as an instructor, create online courses on getting fit.

There is an abundance of money out there in this big wide world. **People don't always buy what they need but they nearly always buy what they want.**

When you provide value and you offer a fair price for giving that value, everyone wins. Why shouldn't you make money from that?

In the next chapter. I'll be giving you the lowdown on creating the perfect balance in your life.

I call it the Golden Triangle.

NO, it's not a Chinese restaurant.

One of my mentors taught me this years ago, and now it's your turn to learn it .

❈ 3 ❈
THE GOLDEN TRIANGLE

How many of us really have true balance in our lives?

If all you have is money and nothing else, your life will always be out of Wack.

There are three Keys to having balance, this forms the Golden Triangle and everyone should learn this.

It's called the Golden Triangle because it consists of three major points, and I believe this information is as valuable as gold.

What has all this got to do with thinking like a Millionaire?

You can have a huge amount of money and be totally miserable. Trust me, I've done it. Without true balance in your life, your life will always feel like you're missing something. On the other hand, you can be relatively low paid and still enjoy your life.

Balance in itself is not very sexy, but it is one of, if not THE key to living a long and happy life.

When you are missing even one of these things, your life will always seem lopsided and it will always feel as if something is missing. It's a bit like trying to drive a car with one wheel missing. This is how many, many people spend their entire lives, totally lopsided.

The 3 Keys to a balanced life.

Step 1. HEALTH

At the top of the triangle is of course, health

This goes without saying, and should always be your No 1 priority. Without good health, it is very difficult to live a good life. However, if you are in bad health at this moment, as long as it isn't terminal, it can nearly always be improved.

This is what you should be working on as the No 1 part of your plan to Wealth.

Health = Wealth.

It's our inner energy that gives us the ideas and action to power up our lives. If your body is always tired, guess what, so will your brain. The brain and the body help each other, but the brain leads the body.

In order to keep the brain and body well, we need plenty of water, good breathing and a diet of good food.

Good health also comes from daily exercise, eating good food in reasonable proportions and feeding your mind good, positive thoughts.

Many people eat nothing but junk food, get little or no exercise and feed their brains daily with televised violence, they get their daily dose of bad news and then they then go and hang out with complainers.

No wonder their life is a mess.

This is a recipe for disaster. You can't operate with an entrepreneurial mind if you are tired or sick all the time.

Check your friends. You are the average of your closest five friends. If you want to start thinking like a Millionaire, get rid of all negative influences. You can't have good thoughts while having bad ones at the same time.

What you eat on a daily basis is either healing you or hurting you, it's either giving you energy or it's sapping energy from you, and possibly slowly destroying you.

I know, these are harsh words. But frankly, if you want to be rich, you have to look the part. It's no good coughing, wheezing and being a slob all over the place. Straighten up, smarten up and look the part.

So, step 1 to a NEW healthy you..

Drink more water, get more sleep.

Eat healthier food, ditch the junk food, ditch the cigarettes, ditch the excessive alcohol intake, walk more, eat only when hungry, stop snacking all day and don't eat two to three hours before bedtime.

Eating before bedtime can contribute towards weight and digestion problems. Plus it can cause lack of sleep as your body is constantly trying to digest your food.

Drink more water, eat more fruit and veg, learn how to breathe better. I can recommend a breathing technique such as the Wim Hoff method (check it out on YouTube).

Create a program every day for looking after YOU.

This is not Rocket science, and it's a well known fact that over 70% of people who end up sick in hospital, are actually there because of bad lifestyle, and bad diet

Don't neglect your body, it's the only one you'll get. You will need that baby to transport you around until you're at least 90. Who knows, maybe for a lot longer if you look after it properly.

I spend time every morning exercising (walking) and also meditating. This helps lower my blood pressure and keeps me in shape.

I cut out a lot of crap like white bread, fries, burgers , etc.

BONUS How I keep in shape and look good without actually going on a diet..

This is something I do every day, however, consult your doctor first if you are on medication or need any medical advice. I am not a doctor or nutritionist, this just works for me.

Skip Breakfast. Eat between 12 noon & 6.30 Each day.

If you still love breakfast, eat it a Midday. This allows your body to be able to rest from breaking down food for approximately 17/18 hrs a day.

Traditionally, people tend to spread their meals around throughout the day, however this can overwork your system, especially if they are big meals, and can cause excessive tiredness. If you eat before bedtime, a lack of sleep can occur.

Your body needs time to rest from digesting food.

Allowing a 17/18hr break daily from digesting food can increase metabolism and reduce your weight.

SIDE-NOTE: Don't resist hunger. If you feel hungry, then eat. But try to stick to a 17/18 Hr break per day. You'll soon notice the difference.

This will give you more energy and help you maintain a lower weight, it could also speed your metabolism up.

What to do next?

Join a health club/ gym. Go for a daily walk or cycle ride. Eat better food, or even join a class that teaches you to cook healthy food.

Hang out with healthy people. Slobs love company, it doesn't mean you have to be one.

(2nd Disclaimer - consult your doctor before making any radical changes).

Remember. In order to think like a millionaire, start to look like one. Don't walk around head down, looking ill and looking like you've got all the problems in the World.

Head up. Eyes forward.

STEP 2. RELATIONSHIPS.

This is so important. Not only the relationships with others, but the relationship that you have with yourself. After all, if you don't like or love yourself, how can you expect other people to like or love you.

Your life is like a mirror, your feelings about yourself are picked up by other people, and they tend to treat you how you see and treat yourself.

If you look comfortable in your own skin, people will warm to you.

I'm not talking about loving yourself in a crazy, scary kind of weird way here. I'm talking about you liking you well enough, that you actually have great respect for yourself, warts and all.

Love yourself for who you are. Trust me, whoever you are, you are good enough. Don't keep beating yourself up for past mistakes, forget them and forgive yourself, (if you need to), and then move on.

Don't play the victim. Sometimes people like to get attention by always playing the victim. You might know someone who is like this.

Victims are drawn to victims, and they will consistently try to keep you a victim too if you're not careful. Neediness is not very attractive. Confidence is.

VICTIM mode is often where a person does not like themselves a whole lot and seeks to grab attention from others to make themselves feel better.

People will never make you happy, only you can make you happy. Yes, people can add to your happiness, but only you can really make you a happy person.

"You are happy the moment you decide you are"

— UNKNOWN

Victims blame their problems on the world, the environment, the government, their spouse, partner, or even their boss, in fact, everyone but themselves..

It's always someone else's fault, according to them.

If you see yourself as a victim, then you are. And so will everyone else. Other "victims" may like you, but you want respect, not sympathy.

People love confident, self-assured people. I'm not talking about arrogance here, I'm talking about that sexy confidence that people just love.

People look up to and follow people who are moving in an upwardly direction. If you are constantly complaining about things and always looking to the negative side, you will turn off a lot of people.

People choose people as friends who are either like them, or people, whom they would like to become.

Not many people like people who play the victim card, exit victim mode as quickly as possible if you are playing that game.

Obviously we need to show empathy to real victims of crime, ill health etc, but don't get sucked into listening to people who are always playing the victim.

Life can be lonely. Choose your friends wisely, a lot of what they say and do will rub off on you, and we all need people, even if we kid ourselves that we don't.

It's a very lonely world without people. And even if you are down and totally friendless at the moment

You can always fix that..

Your true friends will soon come to light when you need help. Ask yourself this question, how many of your friends will just call you up to come and see you, just to find out how you are?.

These are your real friends.

A small group of real friends is much better than a large group of fair weather friends, those are people who only want you around when you're doing something for them.

Get off your butt and join some clubs if you are lonely. Talk to people. Go do the things you like and meet other people who also like doing those things.

People won't come to you. Go out and make it happen.

For example. If you like cooking vegetarian food, go join an evening class, get to meet other like-minded vegetarians.

If you love fishing, join a fishing club. If you love cars, join a car club etc

There are no shortage of great things you can do to meet other people. There is a shortage of people who are willing to make the first move though.

Don't let that be you. For things to change, you have to go out and change them.

I have been on Facebook for 10 yrs now (at the time of writing this book), I can't tell you how many times I've started to chat to people living in an area near me and met up with them for a coffee.

I've established some great friends doing this.

If you wait for others to come to you, you'll probably wait forever. Most people are a little bit scared about making the first move, that's why they don't. It's about you making the move first, this way, you are controlling the situation.

I'm not an outgoing person by nature, but in order to make things happen, i've nearly always made the first move. Sometimes you don't realise how hard it is for some people to act first, many people are actually relieved that you took the time and trouble to make the first move.

This applies to friends, life partners, business partners etc.

Hang out with good people, engage with good people, listen to the encouragers of the world and become one.

You could even try a dating service. There's nothing wrong with this at all, it's not the weak who go to dating services, it's the strong. The people that are taking charge and re-engineering their own future..

Talking about Dating Services..

Here's a Funny Story:

My dad got divorced after 28 years of marriage to my mum (that's not the funny part).

After a couple of years of being on his own, he decides to try a dating service. He gets this date with someone who wasn't really into him at all, so to let him down gently, she gives my dad her sister's number to call.

My Dad calls her sister, her name was Brenda, then goes out on a date with her

He ends up being happily married to her for 28yrs, exactly the same amount of years that he was married to my mum.

Sadly my Dad has now passed away, but I've never forgotten that story..

Was it Fate?

Or was it that he made the first move?. You never know just how your life can change with a phone call or a meeting with the right person at the right time.

There are many clubs, both online and offline for meeting people. Once you get over the initial awkwardness of meeting new people, it will become a breeze.

One of my very good friends loves Salsa dancing. She's single (at this moment in time) and meets a lot of people all over the World through her love of Dancing..

Think about it..

This is an ideal way for men and women to meet lots of people.

Whatever you decide to do, if you hang out long enough with positive people, you will start to think more positively. It also works in reverse of course, if you hang out with negative people..

It rubs off on you..

Make sure the people you hang out with are people who are adding to your life and inspiring you, not the ones sucking the life out of you.

Step 3. MATERIAL WEALTH

This is the 3rd step of the Golden triangle but is obviously very important. And it's really what this book is all about.

Without a roof over your head, it's very hard to be healthy or in a good relationship. Houses cost money, rent cost money.

The same goes for clothes, food, electricity and water. We all need these things to be healthy. And all of these things cost money.

Some people spend their whole lives making a case for not having money. I hate to say this but this usually comes from people who don't have any in the first place. They make endless excuses as to why they don't have any.

I have never understood why people think this way. Money is neither evil nor good, it is just money, a way to exchange value.

People who become rich just become more of what they already were before they had it. A jerk will always be a jerk. But with money, they are now a Rich Jerk

A kind person will always be kind, But they can be kind and rich too, they can be even more kind and generous.

Money doesn't change anyone who doesn't want to be changed.

The next time you hear a person say that money doesn't buy happiness, tell them about the $20,000,000 that a rich philanthropist donated to build a children's cancer ward. I'm sure that made a lot of people happy.

Or the Scholarships awarded by Walmart to poorer folks in downtown New York. That made a lot of people happy.

True, a pile of money won't make you happy.

But, money can buy you things that can make you, your family and friends a whole lot happier. Travel, better healthcare, nicer homes, healthier food, money to give to your favourite causes etc.

It can give you the power to do more good things, give meals to the homeless for example. How about supplying water to a parched African village?, this costs money. You can do all of this when you have it..

SO, sorry to anyone who still thinks money stinks and that it's the root of all evil, it really isn't. This is one of the biggest misquotes of all time, it's the LOVE of money that is actually the root of all evil..

Don't love money, love people.

Money should be something you receive from the value that you give to others. If you're not getting paid much in your job, ask yourself these questions

1. Can just anyone do my job, or is it highly skilled?
2. Are there plenty of people out there looking for a job like this?

You are paid on the perceived value of your service. If you work in McDonalds, your rates of pay are obviously going to be less than for someone who studies for years to become a brain surgeon..

You are getting paid your market rate. The rate of value you give to the marketplace. Whether you agree this is fair or not, it just is.

Just because you work in McDonalds (c), and there's nothing wrong with working in McDonald's, it doesn't mean that you have to stay there for life, you can always upgrade your skills to offer more value to the marketplace..

You could always set up your own McDonald's Franchise, or of course, any other Business you choose.

The Ladder is always more crowded at the bottom than it is at the top. People don't always have the skills, or the confidence to go after the top jobs, and they often see their current job as their actual limit.

This is of course, total tosh, you are NOT your job, it's just a description of what you do, and there are absolutely NO limits for you.

If it's possible, you can do it.

So, there you have it. People will tell you you can't have it all, but you really can.

You can have good health, a great relationship with yourself and others, plus plenty of material wealth all at the same time..

BUT, even though you can have everything, there will be plenty of times when this won't all happen at once. You won't get perfect balance all of the time.

Sometimes, things don't always work out how you expect them to, a business can fail through no fault of yours, (look at the Covid 19 Pandemic of 2020/2021) and sometimes you can enjoy good health, and you might still get ill.

You can be in a great relationship for years, and then. BOOM, all of a sudden it crashes.

The point here is, you can have it all, but you may not be in perfect balance all of the time. Things can go wrong, and when they do, pick yourself up and rise to the challenge.

Live for now. Enjoy your life now.

Again, it's balance that comes to the rescue. When things go wrong, look at what else you have going on in your life and you won't sweat every problem that comes along.

Keep focusing on the good things in your life.

Be thankful, be grateful for what you do have. Being grateful and being grateful with feeling somehow starts to create good things into your life.

Life is full of problems. Our job is to get over them.

So, let me finish this chapter by saying. YES, you can have it all, allow good things to come into your life, you do that by letting go of the bad things in your life.

If your past has been troubling you, let it go and move on.

Stop thinking about things that could go wrong, and concentrate on the things that can go right. Focus on solutions, not the problem.

Your thoughts control your actions. Your actions become your habits, and your habits decide your future.

Whatever your dominant thoughts are, remember that in order to be rich and attract all the money you want, money has got to want to go to you.

First and foremost, Money goes to those who believe they can have it.

Wealth always comes to those who think they are already wealthy.

I know, it sounds crazy but the more you believe you are something, the more it is likely to appear in your life.

You are acting out the feelings of wealth before they actually appear. This is the heart and the brain working together.

You can't attract serious amounts of money with a poverty mindset. You can't be an entrepreneur with an employee mindset. Change your thoughts - change your life.

In the next chapter we're going to be talking about freedom. I think you'll agree, having freedom is something we all would like.

Imagine if you could go anywhere you wanted, do anything you wanted anytime at all and never have to worry about finding the money to finance it.

Wouldn't that be great?

❦ 4 ❦
FREEDOM, THE ULTIMATE HIGH

Why is it some people appear to be living the life of ultimate freedom, whilst others are living lives of struggle and regret?

This is a good question and one that is a mystery to many people.

For centuries people far and wide have sought to be free. Of course, freedom means many things to many people.

What does seem to be clear though is that many employed people are deeply unsatisfied in their jobs. Of all the surveys I've ever seen on "Are you happy at your job" they nearly all seem to be heavily weighted on the dissatisfied side.

Some people love their jobs, and I get that. When I worked in a High Street bookies many years ago I loved it, I couldn't wait to get to work. I was passionate about sports (I still am), so it was heaven getting paid to do something I loved.

But for most people, it's not like that. So, my question to you is, what does freedom mean to you?

Write it down, let it all out. Being clear about something is the first step to obtaining it.

For some people, it could mean financial freedom. Having enough money coming in daily, weekly, etc, so as to no longer have to worry about it.

Many, many relationships have been ruined due to constant arguments about the lack of money.

It is quite common for people to compare themselves to their friends, family and neighbours when it comes to money.

Another aspect of freedom is to have time freedom. Many people are tied to their jobs for 40 to 50 hours a week and they long to escape. When we do this for 40 to 50 years, this is a huge chunk of our lives to give up to work for someone else.

I have spent years in and out of jobs, and although security in a job once existed, it really doesn't exist today, not unless you are in the frontline services or maybe the armed forces.

We risk even more by trying to avoid risk. The premise that a job is safe, just doesn't exist anymore.

I honestly think that leaving something to chance is quite foolish. Especially when we can create new income streams on a part time basis. You don't have to leave your job to create more income, you just have to be creative with your free time.

Let's be honest, living a "normal" life can be pretty stressful. It can be a constant struggle uphill paying bills, and trying to keep house and home together.

We have children, they cost money to feed, clothe and educate. The boss won't give you a raise just because you are now expecting another child. The yearly rise you may get probably won't buy you much, or even match inflation.

Starting a business, whether part-time or full-time is risky, but avoiding that risk altogether could be the riskiest thing you've ever done.

I want you to imagine what freedom means to you. Not just an amount of money, but imagine what that would mean to you and your family.

How does it look?

Maybe it would mean working less hours, making more money, traveling to exotic places, laying on sandy beaches. Maybe it means not having to worry about the cost of things..

Now look at the cost of not doing it?

Each day that you are NOT doing it is another day you DON'T get to enjoy your new free life, keep doing what you're doing now and that day may NEVER come.

You see, when you work out the cost of not doing something, this can sometimes make you rethink your current strategy. I know it did for me.

I used to get up early, go out in the cold to work, queue in traffic, get to work for an ungrateful boss, and for what? Just so I could just about afford the bills and go on holiday once or twice a year.

That's not thriving. That's surviving.

We are told that we live in a free country, however none of us are truly free. We have laws to abide by (of course), we are taxed one way or another from the cradle to the grave.

Death and taxes are certain.

This doesn't in itself take away anything from being free though, it only feels like a problem if we don't have enough money to solve it. Having plenty of money to be able to afford taxes is a good thing, or being able to afford a good accountant to legally avoid some taxes is even better.

I think one of the best definitions of freedom I have ever heard came from one of America's top motivational business speakers, Tony Robbins.

He said.

> "Freedom is being able to do what you want, whenever you want, wherever you want, with whoever you want"

Now, this may not be YOUR definition of freedom at all, but only you know exactly what freedom means to you. This is why you should write down what it means to you.

Go on, write it down, what does freedom mean to you and your family?. Don't miss anything out, include exact numbers.

Now start to work on a plan to get it. Get the pen running and the brain thinking.

Next question.

Can you ever really be truly free ?

Almost..

You can certainly be freer than you currently are.

Yes, you will still have taxes to pay, you will still need to obey the law, but why not, why shouldn't you be free?.

In my opinion, we should be grateful that we have the funds to pay taxes, someone has to pay for the infrastructure that we live in. We need money to pay for the fire service, police service etc.

And as far as the Law is concerned. Let's be thankful that we have it. This helps keep us all safe at night. Without the law, there would be chaos.

And, Big Brother, well, the World is a big place, once you know how to create a life of Freedom, the next step is to enjoy the world. I personally don't inform everyone where I am 24 hours a day and I don't tell people what I'm doing all the time, and I certainly wouldn't pander to the government and their thirst for other people's information.

I have an accountant that deals with my taxes, I speak to her once or twice a year and pay up and when I'm requested to pay tax. When you are self employed there is usually a ton of allowances anyway that you can write off against income.. It's no big deal

So, paying taxes and living within the law are good things that any free citizen should appreciate..

Freedom is having the choice.

"Shall I go to work today, or shall I go to the beach"?

Why is it so many people don't have that Freedom? Well, if you live in the west or many other countries in the world, you probably do have a choice, but very few people take it up.

Unfortunately some countries in the world operate under a dictatorship, whereby people are kept downtrodden and really have none, or very little choice, and very little opportunity for a way out.

However, most countries have many opportunities for people to excel, break the mould and break free from the "Norm"

What is the "Norm"?

Take note: I'm not knocking this, I'm just describing it.

The "Norm" is being like everyone else. Keeping your head down, getting a job, get married or at least get a partner, have 2.5 kids etc, pay the mortgage etc, retire, then expire.

No one knows their sell-by date but many go through life as if they have all the time in the world left.

And again. I'm not knocking it, for a lot of people, this is fine. But for people reading this book, I'm guessing you want a bit more than that.

In school and college, we are taught to believe that to "fit in" is good, and to "stand out" is not so good.

Becoming wealthy is often frowned upon by the teachers and principals as being a "pipe dream" and a far better and safer bet would be to "comply" with the general education curriculum and stick to "what works", (or what they think works).

Wanting to be an entrepreneur and to make money is often considered as being greedy. However, let's remember, it is the entrepreneurs of this world who create the things you buy and these are the people who create most of the jobs.

It's not greed, it's creating value and exchanging it for money.

You either work for an entrepreneur, a government department or a charity, so it amazes me why so many people are always knocking entrepreneurs?, these people are the lifeblood of progress.

Entrepreneurs innovate and create jobs.

My point here is. More money can equal more choice in life. I've been broke and I've also been quite wealthy, wealthy is a lot better.

Being broke helps no one, least of all, yourself. The best way to help the poor is to not be one. This way you can financially help the poor.

Also, if no one ever "stood out" there would be no leaders, no great inventors, no great artists, no great sports people etc.

Seeking freedom is now even higher on people's shopping list as they get more and more disillusioned with the current system of "work till you drop"

Warning. This might SHOCK you.

The alarming thing about retirement is:

One in five men, and one in eight women don't actually make it to retirement age, they die beforehand. So, they are never able to draw a pension (2).

64% of Americans who do reach retirement age, retire broke (3)

You must admit. The odds are "not good" if you stick to the conventional system.

Then along came the Internet. The Internet changed the whole world. People can now easily work from home and have customers in many countries, all without leaving their homes.

To be free, you have to do things that ordinary people won't, or don't do. And that takes a total switch in a person's mindset.

If you keep on doing the same things, you will keep getting the same things. That is a FACT.

Most conventional wisdom is flawed. Working for someone else for Forty or Fifty years may have seemed a good idea at the time, but as time goes on, you spend your life hoping and praying for a pay rise, hoping for promotion..

Hope is not a Winning strategy.

You can, and must take charge of your own life. Don't leave it until it's too late to create the freedom you want.

You are the only person who can make yourself free. Instead of relying on a boss and helping someone else to build THEIR own dream, why not build your own?.

If you want more, you have to be more. You have to add more value to the Marketplace in order to elevate your standard of living. Having more money creates more freedom.

I know you want more.. This book has the answers. Each chapter builds toward having it all, and believe me, you so deserve it.

Imagine working from home, on the internet bringing in residual income, this type of income is the type I LOVE and you will too. Residual income comes in day after day even when you are not at your desk, in your house or even in the country..

This can all be yours. It's the first step to freedom.

To start thinking like a Millionaire, you need to look at how they, themselves think. I've never heard a Millionaire who constantly complains. I've never heard a Millionaire hoping for the best. Hope isn't a sound strategy.

Millionaires are Pro Active. They seize (or create) opportunities. They think positive, they are relentless, they never give up.. if things are not going to plan. they simply re-adjust their course as they go,

Start to flip that switch in your head, re-adjust your current thinking.

What is the reason you want to be rich?. Think about this for a moment. YES, of course everyone will say it's for the money, but once you have the money, what will you do with it?

What parts of your life will you change?, what will you keep?. How will you spend the rest of your life?, write it all down, start to imagine your new rich life, how does it feel, the more you think about it, the more you'll start to get ideas in your head on how to get it.

The next chapter is a strange one. When I was a kid I was always ducking and diving, trying new ways to make money. But I had a realization of why I was like I was, and maybe you have your own story like this.

What was your defining moment?. What made you want to become rich?. write it all down.. See you in the next chapter.

OK, just a quick reminder. I have a great free gift waiting for you at https://keitheverett.co.uk/special

5

THE MAGIC HOUSE

What was your inspiration to become an entrepreneur? What sparked you wanting to make a better life and get rich?

For me it was the magic house. this is a weird story, I know, it sounds like a fairytale but it is 100% true.

Many years ago, while I was still in short trousers. My Dad summoned me to do some clearing up at my deceased grandfather's house. I think he thought it would be a fun, learning experience for me.

I was probably around 5 years of age but can't remember exactly..

I never knew my grandfather, I'd never met him, but something told me that he was perhaps a bit eccentric or maybe even a little bit cuckoo.

I mean that with the greatest respect, but when I visited his house that day, it all seemed a little bit weird.

As my dad and I entered the old house. I caught sight of the overgrown and untidy trees and bushes out the back, the garden hadn't been worked on for a long time and the old wooden sheds were tumbling down.

This was a very big house, my Grandad was very old when he passed, it was obvious he couldn't look after it as well as he had in his earlier years..

It's quite strange how although we can't always remember everything long term, some things can impact us forever. This was one of those defining moments for me.

I think as small children, we are quick to see the wonder in things. This is something many of us lose as adults, which is a shame. Life through the eyes of a child can be a magical thing.

So, back to the house..

It had tumbled down potting sheds, a greenhouse with no glass and treasure, yes, treasure everywhere, well it looked like that to me.

My Grandfather had been a keen collector of treasure, coins, notes, pearl handled penknives, tins, old medals, toy metal cars you name it, it was there.

He did a lot of digging in those days and I'm not talking about planting seeds, I'm talking about burying things such as money in the garden, and hiding lots of things in that big old house of his.

Clearly, he knew a lot about hidden assets, he hid his very well.

There were coins, and notes. You name it, he buried it..

My Dad gave me the job of clearing out the cupboards at first, I wasn't very tall so I needed the assistance of a stool.

Most people kept food and kitchen utensils in the kitchen, my grandad kept tins, some contained old food, things like biscuits etc but in nearly every cupboard, there were items of interest.

Penknives, medals, old tin toys, and cash.

This was my first attraction to shiny objects, something of a tradition that carried on for many years later when the Internet arrived. I would like to say that my grandad was a keen gardener, but clearly he wasn't.. In place of flowers and plants, he buried tins of treasure instead..

I know money doesn't grow on trees, but I think my grandad's garden may have been the exception. I didn't know much about my grandad but I have a strong feeling he never really trusted banks. A lot of people of this era (1950/60's) were the same. They kept money all over the place, in tins, etc.

He was indeed, a man of mystery...

Back then I was too young to understand, and most of this is a distant memory now, but I will always remember how this early event changed me in my later life..

Was my Grandad CRAZY?, or just careful?.

Well, I guess we'll never know, but one thing always stuck in my head. I loved the idea of accumulating things. And if you're going to accumulate things, it may as well be things of value.

So..

Although my Dad never let me keep the stash, apart from a couple of rusty pennies and maybe a penknife or two, It did trigger something deep down inside of me.

I started to think like a collector, a collector of shiny things. A sort of a Treasure hunter.

If my Grandfather could accumulate all this wealth and hide it in the house, perhaps I too could also be a treasure hunter.

For years after the event, and to this very day, I can always remember those wonderful feelings of that Magical house.

What about you?, what made you want to be a collector of treasure, or a modern-day entrepreneur?, was it the money, the shiny objects, or perhaps the freedom? Maybe it was all three.

Get ready for the next adventure on your journey.. onwards and upwards.

6

THE ART OF RICH THINKING

The first step toward creating richer thinking comes from a little word called Obsession.

This is something every millionaire has in their mental toolbox.

Now, normally when people talk about this word, they tend to talk about it in a very negative way. After all, thoughts of obsession conjure up things like gambling, alcohol, stalking, drugs, etc.

Isn't obsession some kind of madness?

Well, yes, and no.

The trick is to make the madness work for you. If obsession can make you sick, couldn't it also make you well too?, couldn't it also make you rich?

Yes, it can. Not many people talk about this, but a healthy dose of obsession can in fact change your life for the better.

Sometimes, you just need to become obsessed with things before you can get things done. Riches are and have never been created by accident. Success never has or never will just come to you. You have to go to it.

I see a lot of people, especially on the internet looking to do as least as possible to gain the most as possible. This is never going to work.

This goes totally against nature. Nature works by giving and growing. This is how you get rich.

You give great value, and you grow in the process

Everything you do has a knock-on effect. The more you do in the right direction, the greater that effect becomes.

Most Successful Entrepreneurs are 100% obsessed with what they do. It's all about creating opportunities, not waiting for them to come to you.

"All things come to those who wait" is the worst quote i've ever heard. The only things that come to those who wait, are old age and death.

Obsession needs to have legs, we need to create the action needed to get the things that we obsess about.

It works in reverse too. If you obsess about things going wrong, they often will. It's like a magnet, you draw bad things to you as well as good things when you use this great power of obsession.

Just like my grandfather planting money all over the place, he was obsessed either with planting money (unlikely) or with hiding money away from prying eyes.

So, get obsessed. Get obsessed with the results you want. If you want more money then get obsessed with making it. And although I'm talking about an obsession, I'm not talking about doing it to the detriment of your health or your relationships.

You need both of these things onside with you, when embarking on your journey to wealth.

The more you focus, obsess and take action on your goals, the more likely you are to achieve them.

It's not unusual to see obsession at the forefront of society. People obsess about work, what's on TV, personal relationships etc, etc. Life can be a drama.

It takes large steps to create big things. Forget the small stuff.

I can't tell you how many times I've asked people what they want and they say something really obscure like " I just want to make more money"

Without knowing exactly what you want, it's almost impossible to get it.

You have to know exactly what you want. Just wanting money won't get you more money. You have to know exactly what you want, and exactly what value you will create for others in order to get it.

Be EXACT. Start to write this stuff down and get a feel for your ongoing plan.

The money is already made, you don't need to make it, you just need to go out and get it.

Create a plan and stick to it.

The Internet is full of advice. Some good, some bad, however, you have to take that information, personalize it to your own style and create a plan of your own doing. Don't just copy and paste what other people are doing.

We are all followers for a while, it's how we learn, but there is no need to follow forever, take the bull by the horns and start to become a leader. Don't wait for people to tell you what to do.

You want to be original, originality is what sells, if you are just a carbon copy of someone else, you won't create the flow and excitement, to inspire others to do business with you.

Step 1. Ignore the Hype

The very first thing I would say to you is to STOP listening to all the BS you hear, mainly online, about making money.

The Internet is overpopulated with words such as "Free", "Easy", "Autopilot", Copy & Paste", Business in a Box, etc, etc. Indicating that it is the simplest thing in the world to start and succeed in an online business.

I've got news for you. It's NOT!

Trust me on this, it's hard work. It took me years to figure out how to make money on the Internet.

Of course, the concept sounds easy, find a product or service and just sell it.. But in reality, it's not as easy as it sounds. You need customers to buy from you, and this is mainly where people fail. You need enough people to buy from you to make it all worthwhile. I've found this out the hard way.

Build a better mousetrap and people will come?, eh, no, actually they won't.

You have to create customers. Get good at marketing. Any profitable online business is about 90% selling, and 10% creative and technical.

Get selling, as early as possible in your new business.

Get rid of the idea that people just come to you and buy your stuff if you put up a website. It doesn't happen. You have to go out and get the traffic.

Even if you own the best brand in the world, you still have to market it to the masses. Why do you think Coca Cola has so much advertising around the world when they already have the Number one Cola brand?

It's because they have to constantly remind people that they are still there, or people will be sneaking off to buy Pepsi.

Without sales, any business is dead in the water. This is why a lot of people fail, they spend too much time on trimming the bushes, basically putting correct images on to their websites, spellchecking, asking people which colours work, does my logo look right?, etc, etc. I think you get what I mean...

People spend a lot of time time dilly-dallying instead of actually getting sales. A business is only a business once it gets sales. Profit is the be all and end all of it, if you don't make a profit then you just have an expensive hobby.

Of course we need things to look nice and dandy but the only thing that brings money into your business is sales. Figure out how to sell one item, then scale it up to hundreds, thousands, or even millions, that's how to get rich.

I've had some really good successful businesses over the years, but also I've had plenty that have tanked and lost money. The ones that failed miserably, were the ones I didn't focus a hundred percent on. I didn't hustle enough, they just became expensive hobbies.

Many people on the Internet try to start multiple businesses all at once and wonder why they fail. This is because their attention is scattered. Yes, many millionaires have several sources of income, but not from the very beginning.

Concentrate on one business and do it well

In an Online Business, the success rate is only around about 3 to 5%. In a Brick and mortar business, only around 4% of people who start a Business, are still trading in their 2nd year..

This is SHOCKING

That means that 96% of offline businesses fail in the first year and approximately 95-97% of online businesses do the same.

Why is this?

One of the most common reasons for failure is not having a proper plan, not having a sensible business idea, or not realising the scale of work involved, or not actually realising the costs involved.

I've had so many messages online from people who think starting a business should be free, or at least very cheap. I'm here to tell you, if you want to make money, you have to invest money in yourself and your business.

Don't keep looking at making a lot of money through cheap eyes. It takes both time and money to make it big.

You will never know everything about your business. The day you stop educating yourself, is the day you and your business will start declining. Keep learning.

What about a Franchise?

With a Franchise, the Success rates are much higher, however, so are the start up costs. The actual cost of starting a Franchise can be extremely high. For a standard Branded Pizza franchise you are easily looking at $250,000+ and for a McDonalds Franchise you could be looking at $1 Million +

With brick and mortar businesses, including Franchises, you have staff to hire and pay, stock to purchase, plus all kinds of other fees such as leases, franchise fees etc.

I like to keep things simple. Sell online, preferably digital products, as you have no stock to carry and very little staff (if any) are required at first.

And that's why you don't see everyone starting a business. Many people are not cut out for it because it means creating a much better version of the current you. It takes work.

Determination and pure grit are far better attributes than just talent alone. There are plenty of talented people in this world who are broke.

Learn more to become more.

Only recently I purchased a Publishing course, this gave me the knowledge I needed to be successful at publishing books, kindles and audios. The cost justified the results.

You need to invest in yourself.

The average person won't spend time learning and implementing what they learn, as it takes time, money and real effort. This is why most people stick with jobs. It's easier. All they have to do is show up and get paid.

Most people work just hard enough to NOT get fired.

However, although I've had jobs in the past, in my view most jobs STINK.

Here's why

NO job is truly safe in this world

You are not being paid what you are truly worth, you are only being paid what the going market rate allows. Every company needs to make a profit from your labour, therefore you are being paid just enough to stop you from quitting.

You won't get rich in a job unless you are earning at least multiple six figures a year. And even then, after tax it will still take you several years.

Also there are NO tax advantages to be had by being in a job, like there are when you have your own business. The taxman grabs his share of your pay, before you even see it.

It's really about taking back control, obviously the more you rely on other people, the less control you will have over your own life.

At first, you do need to put in a lot of time and effort getting your business off the ground. To start with, it will feel like a job, but without hardly any pay.

You will probably exchange 40 hours a week in a job for 80 hours a week in a business. Relax, this won't be the case forever, sometimes I only work a couple of hours a day in my business, but it wasn't like that in the early days.

I slaved away at the computer all day and sometimes long into the night.

The Trick to making money is not to sit on your cheeks and think about it for months, or years. Decide which business is right for your personality, work out what funds you will need to get started and how much work and effort you will need to put in to get the results you actually want.

Entrepreneurs are always looking forward into the future.

It's really simple..

Business, no matter whether it's a service business or one that supplies products, it's simply a supply and demand business.

Just because you like trainers with Bunny pics on them, doesn't mean everyone else does.. You find something that people want and then you sell it to them.

Don't make it more complicated than it is. Sure, it's nice to sell things that you love, but at the end of the day, give people what they want, give them good products at a good price.

The Niche that you choose to sell in, MUST have room for repeat business, or your business will end up sinking faster than the Titanic.

Repeat business is everything. When you go into a barbers to get a haircut, you don't just go once. If everyone only ever had one haircut the barbers would go broke.

You sell to people over and over again.

Even if the product you sell is a high ticket item and the profit margin is huge, you still want to get more sales from each customer in the form of "up-sells" These are additional sales to the customer in the form of add ons, accessories or even a monthly subscription services.

This keeps the money coming in, and the cashflow healthy.

Repeat sales are the lifeblood of any business.

SO, YES be passionate about your business. After all, you're going to be joined at the hip with it for many years to come.

But, before you decide on the method of selling, online, MLM, affiliate marketing, dropshipping, selling on eBay © Amazon © etc, decide on this.

What Micro-niche (a Niche broken down into a sub niche) is not being catered for properly out there?

In what micro niche could I get a large piece of the pie in?

For example. Health and wellness may be a good niche, but it's very broad and loaded with competition. But health and wellness for the over 50's is a far more targeted, micro-niche.

Micro-niches can be very profitable, as there is far less competition, and you have a greater chance of dominating them. Don't just target anyone and everyone.

What products are there within this micro niche of yours, and are they in demand?

Let me give you an example..

Let's say you are a gun fanatic, you love shooting clay pigeons, this is also your passion.

You find out that there is this special gun which is so accurate, even your cross-eyed friend could hit the target every time.

So, you ask yourself, "what else will people who buy this gun, actually buy?

They will probably buy a case to look after it

They will probably buy a cleaning kit to clean it

They will definitely buy shells

They will probably buy clay pigeons

They may even buy a monthly membership to your very own gun club

They may even pay for shooting lessons.

Do you see where I'm going with this? If they like you, and you give them great value, they will keep buying shells and clay pigeons from you forever.

A quick note from me:

Always, always, always sell products or services that give value to people. People will only buy Junk once, and then probably ask for a refund. That customer is then lost forever.

Bad news spreads fast, good news takes a while.

Lead with value. Offer people exceptional customer service, and look after your customers.. They in return will love and look after you .

On to our next chapter..

7

JUST DO IT

I know Nike says "Just Do it", and it's a simple statement but of course, it's also very powerful.

There could be 101 reasons why people don't "Just Do It", some make perfect sense, others of course can just be excuses. In fact, if we make enough of them, those excuses become a habit and we just procrastinate about everything, as our subconscious mind now thinks it's normal to put things off.

Decisions then become more difficult to make.

Sometimes it's just a plain old lack of money, a lack of knowledge, or even a lack of motivation, you name it and a million people have used it before.

This "lack of [insert excuse here]" won't of course stop the most determined person. We need to start asking ourselves a different question. Instead of saying "I Can't", let's start asking ourselves "How Can I?"

In order to think like a millionaire, we have to be honest with ourselves. Some of the highest paid people in the land have all used some form of excuse at some time or other. I've made plenty of them myself, but I eventually swapped my excuses for action.

However, no matter how much of a real or not so real an excuse it is, we simply have to get around it, over it, or even go through it.

The time is never going to be right. Your ducks will never all be in a row. One thing is for sure though, time will eventually run out for all of us.

Acknowledge your fear by all means, but do it anyway.

The thing is, the time will never be perfect, nor will you. We have to start imperfectly and adjust as we go, or the truth is, it just won't happen.

NO Money? – Find a way to get some. If you want to be a Millionaire, you can't let the lack of money stop you. Hustle and save. When the right opportunity comes along, be prepared to go in all guns blazing. That means be prepared to invest.

NO Time? – Quit doing things that aren't bringing you closer to your goal. Start putting time aside for things that really matter.

Thinking of all the things that could go wrong? - NOTHING in life is certain, take a chance, what's the worst thing that can happen?

You can't go through life being afraid. We all end up doing things we don't like at times. We all have problems, and many millionaires were in fact broke at the very start. The difference is, they got started and kept going.

OK, I admit, I hate washing up, I can't stand cleaning up the house, but I do it. Why?, because I don't want to live in a pigsty - Simple..

This is why I do anything. If I don't, things will just get worse. Inaction is a curse.

Many of the people I know online are earning six figures. Several are earning 7 figures or more. What would have happened if they had just decided to get a job and said" To hell with working for myself" it's too hard?

Answer: They would never have been able to give their family the lifestyle they have now. They would probably have spent their entire lives worrying about money and always trying to play catch up when paying the bills.

The pain of not doing something can be a lot greater than actually doing it. This is what causes people to take quick and drastic action to change their lives.

Don't fear change, it's the driving force behind success. **Without it you're screwed.**

For things to change, you have to take drastic action, now. Right now..

You need to create new habits, if your current habits are not serving you, change them.

Today you can make that start. Even if it's just a few baby steps forward, it's a start.

We are always learning. The day we stop learning is the day that we die. Sure, we can go to seminars, webinars and read books all day, but the best education comes from doing.

Doing creates the motivation to keep on doing. And by doing and adjusting as we go, we get the results we want.

Most people know what to do, but they don't do what they know.

The stars will never align correctly, all you can do is decide that now is the right time, now is the only time.

Are entrepreneurs born or made?. The answer is both. Not everyone is a natural entrepreneur, but anyone can grow into becoming one.

I have had the entrepreneurial spirit in me ever since I was a small boy. Ever since I first came across my dear old grandfather's garden of buried treasure.

Not everyone is a natural entrepreneur. That's OK. You can do anything if you are willing to change your mindset.

You change you mindset by thinking, then doing more of what will get you nearer to your goal, and thinking and doing less of what's been stopping you.

People call me lucky. I've had several businesses, many worked out, many didn't. It wasn't luck. I simply made myself do it.

I didn't create any of these situations by thinking about them. You don't create a baby, by just thinking about it.

I created them by doing it, I felt fearful, at first, but then I just took action. I adjusted as I went along. Mistakes and failures are just speed bumps along the road to success. When/if it all goes wrong, you adjust and keep going.

It's all really a beautiful game. Just like chess.

Keep this book with you always. Read and reread it. If you have friends that you truly care about and they too want to create a money consciousness, buy them a copy. Don't part with yours, don't lend it, you may never see it again.

The Myths about Making Money

Obviously everyone has an opinion on just how easy or hard it is to make money. People peddle all kinds of magic solutions on the Internet, many of which can be downright misleading and unlawful.

Money, or the lack of it, is perhaps one of the biggest problems people face throughout their lives apart from bad health. People generally exchange a huge portion of their life working for the man, or woman in order to make life more comfortable.

But being comfortable won't make you rich. You need to welcome the uncomfortable, get comfortable with being uncomfortable - it's a price you pay now to get rich in the future.

Let's be honest, the old 40 to 50 hour weeks working for others for 40 to 50 years is never going to make anyone rich. If anything it only makes people tired and cynical, it does however pay the bills.

BUT, were you born just to pay bills?

Each and every one of us has probably been in a job at some stage of our lives, I've had many, but you don't need to stay there and give up such a HUGE chunk of your life working for others.

I used to work for a Bus company in Essex, England. I would pick up one of the supervisors in my car every morning and take him into work.

He used to love talking about his two houses. He had one that he rented out in the North of England and one that he lived in, in the South of England.

He worked hard, he had been at the company for over 30 years. He was due for retirement in a few short weeks. He told me he was selling the house he had rented out in the North and was looking forward to a good retirement.

He was going to enjoy his retirement with the money from the house sale.

On his last day at the work he had a heart attack and died. He had literally spent his life working for others and never had a chance to enjoy his retirement.

The reason I'm telling you this is because more people have a heart attack early Monday morning than at any other time because of the stress of going to work.

Don't be one of them.

A job will pay the bills, but it needn't be a life sentence.

The problem lies in the human psyche, most people don't think that they are good enough to go out and make it on their own, hence they stick with a "safe" job. However as we discussed earlier in this book, no job is really that safe, not nowadays.

Being an entrepreneur does involve an element of risk, not everyone is able or willing to take those risks, however we all take risks every day, even just getting to and from our jobs is a risk.

If you drive for a living or you drive to work, you are taking the risk that someone coming in the opposite direction won't drive into you and harm, or kill you. There is risk everywhere.

Unmanaged risk.

Life is a risk. Not taking risks is a very risky strategy in itself, Don't bank on winning the lottery, the odds of doing so are horrendously low.

In my country (England), the odds of winning our biggest lottery is 14,000,000 Million to one. The odds of starting a business and it actually working out long term are approximately 20/1.

Those odds are a lot better.

Money comes to those who actively create systems for giving great value to people, in exchange for money.

I've traded on the Internet since 2004 selling physical products, and I've also been a digital marketer (a person who sells digital products) since 2010.

I've seen many schemes and scams come and go, but the truth is, most people selling on the Internet are actually law abiding people just like you and me who want to make money to help support their families, and live a better life.

Of course there are crooks and conmen in almost any trade, ranging from the builders from hell to online Ponzi schemes and Pyramids.

You do have to be careful, but being over careful can lead you to never take chances. It's a fine balance between taking calculated risks or never taking a chance on anything at all.

Let's look at making money in simple terms.

You decide on what products or service you want to sell

You market the products or service

You collect the money

This of course is only the basics. Where it all goes wrong is when people try to over complicate things. There is a course for almost everything online, and many people believe they need all the pieces in place before they can begin their business. They watch endless amounts of webinars, read countless courses and think they've done enough.

Although education is good, action is where all the money is. You won't get paid for attending webinars or reading books.

Taking unorganised action is often a lot better than taking NO action at all. I do this all the time.

I am in a constant mode of experimentation. Half the time, I don't exactly know what i'm doing, I have an idea, I start to do it, and I learn as I go.

Knowledge is only power if you actually do something with it. If it stays in your head, it's not a lot of good to you, except to show how clever you are.

There are a lot of very clever people in the cemetery who died without taking action on what they know. They lived their whole life with plans in their head, but they never took the action to bring their dreams to life.

Wishing is a fools game. Doing is the game of Pro's

OK, let's look at some more Myths about Making Money.

One common myth is that it's not possible to start a business if you have a job, a life partner, kids, a mortgage and lots of debt.

This is total rubbish..

This is a favourite excuse from several of my friends. The trouble with this is, it is completely false.

Usually, the conversation starts with "It's alright for you", you are (fill in the blanks). This really is just them projecting their reasons for not starting anything on to you, and why you have all the advantages that they don't.

The truth is, they wish for things, but you go out and actually make it happen.

You can dress things up any way you want, but if something is a wish, it won't get done. If you've 100 percent made up your mind to do something, then no one on earth can stop you.

Entrepreneurs are and always have been people of all types. Some are married, some have partners, some have kids, pets and mortgages.

There is no "one size fits all" when it comes to an entrepreneur.

The most common excuse for not starting a business is "When I get home from work I'm too tired". Yes, the reason you are too tired in the first place is because you work all day for someone else.

Work for yourself part time, evenings and weekends..

I've personally found from coaching hundreds of people that many of them want to get started but they spend a lot of time convincing themselves it can't be done.

People are often their own problem.

They genuinely think their reasoning to not get started is real. The truth is, you can either make money or you can make excuses.

People program themselves for failure every day. Don't let this be you. You bought this book because you want more. Now is the time to break the mould and BE more.

Your partner/spouse will need to be on your side of course. If they want a better life, they need to support you. If not, sometimes you just have to go out and do it regardless.

Keep it simple, but more importantly

Get Started...

YES, right Now!..

In the next chapter we are going to look at how the crazy world we live in creates generation after generation of delusional people. This is HOT!

8

THE WEIRDNESS OF LIES

Much of what you see in "real life" is actually an illusion.

Take Social Media for instance. This gives people an opportunity to portray the life that they want to show to the world. It's so easy these days to make it look like you're doing really well, when the truth might be quite a lot different.

Social media gives people significance, which of course is something we all want.

You can find a Lamborghini parked in the street, take a selfie by it, pretend it's yours. Find a nice house, take a selfie, pretend it's yours. See how easy it is to give people the impression that you are doing really well in life?

This is both true, and perhaps a little sad.

We are who we are. We should all be very proud of that. Faking it while you make it might work for some, but how many of those people are actually making it while they're faking it?

Looking the part is not the same as being the part. .

What works a whole lot better, in my opinion is to tell your story, warts and all. People love a good story, and if your story is one of struggle, from which you overcome and emerge victorious. People will love that.

The truth is, most people who have acquired wealth, tend not to tell the world about it. After all, if you keep bragging or boasting, someone will eventually try to burgle your house or steal your car. Perhaps even both..

Of course, there are always exceptions, some people just don't care and will flaunt their wealth anyway.

The sad part is, many people feel they have to pretend they are doing well, as they aren't really satisfied at all with their life. This is a shame.

People are not always who they appear to be, and sometimes it's tough knowing who is actually genuine and who isn't.

It's a crazy world we live in, full of fake news, celebrities who are only famous for being famous. However it is up to us to make sense of it all. Only when we take charge of our own lives can we really focus on living a better one.

The point I'm making here is that we should not compare ourselves to other people EVER. You never really know how much a person has struggled to get to where they are today.

Yes, it's true. for some people, life is easy. But for most, it's a struggle. It's mainly a struggle though because many people are dealing with their inner demons inside on a daily basis, whilst trying to cope with the world outside.

When we see others doing well, we tend to compare ourselves with them, without giving any thought to how long that person may have been struggling before actually achieving the results that they have today.

It's rather like comparing apples to oranges. We often don't compare actual like, with like.

I know you may hate to hear this but your life is ebbing away. Comparing yourself to others is such a time wasting activity. It's almost criminal.

Be happy with you.

Let's concentrate on the time we have left in our lives and make full and proper use of that time.

Don't sell yourself short or beat yourself up for past failures. You are much better than that. We nearly always underestimate ourselves, and quite often sell ourselves short.

You have probably heard people talk about "biding their time", or doing something to "pass the time". This is crazy thinking. Time is the most valuable commodity we have apart from oxygen, water & food.

Why would you want to just pass the time?, surely time is there for us to go out and live to the fullest. Biding time is really just wasting time, isn't it?

Value your time. It's worth a whole lot more than money. You can always get more money, but you can't get more time.

You can save time. But you can't make more of it. When your time comes to bite the bullet and meet the grim reaper, trust me all the money in the world is not going to save you.

Life really is an optical illusion. Everyone sees the world differently. We all have our own version of the truth.

Just because the majority say something, it doesn't mean that it's true. In 2020/2021, during the great Pandemic there were so many conflicting messages going around between certain health authorities and government ministers.

Everyone seemed to have a different version of the truth.

It all got very confusing. Even the media got in on the act to portray their version of the facts.

People lie. It's a fact. Yes even trusted people do it.

The truth was someone's opinion, that got verified by the majority somewhere along the line in history, and it got marked down as a fact. When a large group of people agree on something, it tends to be perceived as the truth, after all the majority are always right aren't they?

Eh. No.

Because something is perceived as the truth doesn't mean it is actually right?.

Entrepreneurs are people who observe the rules, but don't always follow them. They tend to question things more closely and never wildly believe things just because a person in authority said it.

Time and time again politicians have been caught lying through their teeth and twisting the facts.

However, it is not the majority of people who are out there living the best lives. The majority of people are just getting by. This is a fact that actually is true.

Question everything. Is the news we see on TV actually the truth or is it the News' channels version of the truth?.

Does the leader of your country always tell the truth?

Is every diagnosis from a reputable doctor always accurate?

You see what I mean here. It's best to double check everything, and then make your own mind up.

At some stage, people believed in Witches. In fact, Witches were so feared that people used to burn them. This was their truth at the time, of course today, we now have a much different view.

What happened?

The TRUTH changed.

As far as I know, this is the only time we will be here, we are all just passing through this life. Life as you know, is a journey

We could all do so much more if we would only wake up to it.

We are living in a "no holds barred" world now. Absolutely anything is possible. Anyone who can drag themselves away from the TV set can get a business going and improve their lot.

And long may it last..

Remember, you're not going to live forever. Don't die without truly living. Awaken that sleeping spirit within you. Become a master of something and monetize the hell out of it to create a better life for you and your family.

NOT giving up when you want to is half of it, too many people just pack it in at the wrong time and never ever reach the heights they want to.

It's always going to be a lot easier to just not bother or to give up halfway through something, but it is those relentless people who just keep on going who achieve greatness, you don't have to be a magician to create MAGIC, but you do have to keep going, even when that little voice inside keeps telling you to quit.

Keep pushing for Greatness!!

See you in the next chapter.

/ 9 /

THE MILLIONAIRE BUSINESS MODEL

There is a Jungle out there and do you know what?, it's something that most people bungle, it's called The Money Jungle..

Some people are always struggling with money, some are happy with what they have and then there are others who are always trying to make more.

How much is enough money? Jeff Bezos has more money than anyone on the planet, but he still wants more. I don't think anyone has the right to tell anyone that they have too much.

Some people are a lot more ambitious than others. I never feel guilty about making money and you shouldn't either.

After all, people who make a lot of money tend to be big consumers, which is good for the economy, plus they often end up employing people.

They also tend to give more to charity.

Everyone looks at the art of making money differently. Some go the job route, some go the entrepreneurial route, some go the investment route, whilst others go the artist, author, songwriter, singer or pro sports route.

Whatever route you go, it will obviously impact the amount of money you make. A person who works 40 hours a week for $10 an hour would obviously find it extremely difficult to become a millionaire unless they altered this path in some way.

Jobs are only the starting point.

I have spent many years as a person in a job, but I never became my job. You also are not your job, you are someone who is in a job. This needn't define who you are. This is very important, as we live in a world where everyone wants to label us.

When I was scraping a living driving a bus, I never once considered myself as a "Bus Driver". I considered myself as an entrepreneur who was simply driving a bus to make a living.

What do you do for a living?

How you answer this determines how people treat you. This is the way of the World, what you do, even the car you drive, it all drives people's opinions of you.

If you see yourself as your job title, the chances are you'll grow into that title and may pursue that job forever. Some people are quite content to be in the same job for 30 or 40 years or more.

I'm not saying that there is anything wrong with that, but if your intention is to get rich, and I assume it is, as you are reading this book, a change of thinking is rapidly required.

The Jungle is a vast wasteland.

This wasteland is really the Jungle of wasted lives. People who could have, but didn't quite. People who were always going to press the button but didn't quite get around to it. Time caught up with them and then BOOM!!

They got ejected from this life, their sell-by date arrived and all bets are off, all opportunities are gone. This is sad, but true.

As people get older both in age and in mind, they tend to settle for "the lot" they have.

This might be you..

I have some great news for you..

Anyone can change in a moment, even in a heartbeat. You are not stuck, you only think you are. Everyone feels they are stuck in a rut at some stage, the good thing is, you don't have to stay stuck.

And this stupid age thing. People make so much out of being a certain age. Age will only be a factor if you let it, many millionaires did not become so until they reached their fifties, sixties or seventies.

Who says, you can't get rich at eighty?

Sure, you might slow down a bit, but as long as your brain hasn't gone to sleep or died, you are good to go.

"If you think you can, or if you think you can't, you are probably right"

— HENRY FORD

Henry Ford said this many years ago and it still runs true today.

It's all in your head. What goes on inside your head influences your outer World.

Most people won't flip the switch in their brain until they absolutely have to.. When they're backed into a corner, or if they get fired for instance, or if they get sick and tired of being sick broke and tired.

Here is how you flip that switch in your head..

Step 1. Always think you can. Even if you don't know how to yet

Step 2. Instead of thinking "I can't" think "how can I?"

Step 3. Always remember, failure is part of the winning process, show me someone who hasn't failed and I'll show you someone who has done very little in life.

Step 4. Give your ideas the action they deserve, and if you are short on ideas, go where people with all the ideas hang out, Forums, Facebook groups, YouTube etc. There are no shortage of good people out there who are willing to share ideas with you.

Hopefully you see how simple it is to be a part of a more positive movement. It all begins with how you think, who you hang out with and how much you are willing to improve.

How do you view the world?. Do you see it as friendly place, or somewhere that is hostile? How you answer that question will determine how you think and what actions you take.

You can't be fearful and positive at the same time. It's like mixing hot chillies with strawberries.

Stay away from toxic people, they only see gloom and doom in everything and everyone. I swear there are people out there who actually enjoy being negative.

The Millionaire Business Model

I'll even give you a vehicle to make money right now. This works for me and it'll work for you too, no matter if you are a young person or someone who is in their late 70's, 80's or 90's, this just flat out works for everyone.

The Problem Solving Business

Facts are Facts. People have problems.

More and more people are joining the super rich by copying this business model.

Problems are wonderful, honestly.

To most people problems are very negative, however to the entrepreneur, you, and me, people's problems give us an unlimited production line of opportunities. People with problems need answers, they need solutions, and most people want them right NOW! Instantly downloadable.

The world is short of, and always will be, good problem solvers. Problem-solving is at the very peak of the reason why anyone buys anything at all, think about it.

What's In It For Me?.

When someone buys a pack of disposable razors, they don't buy them because they like shaving, they buy them because they don't like a hairy face, armpits or legs.

So, think of all the problems that people face on a daily basis in the World. There are thousands of them, and each and every day, new ones come along.

You make money by being the solution. People pay for solutions.

Now, you might be saying to yourself. "This guy is nuts. I can't solve my own problems, let alone anyone else's".

OK, let's start with yours..

What problems do you have?

I bet.. There are other people who have the exact same problems as you. One of the reasons we are all alike in this world is that we all have problems. Rich or poor, we still, all have problems.

Find out how to solve that problem, and then sell them the solution.

Solutions can be sold to a global audience on the Internet in either the form of a short report, a Kindle eBook or even a paperback book. It may even be a whole course.

That's literally what I do. Create Digital products that solve problems.

Now, before you say "I'm hopeless at writing" – Think BIG.

Even if you haven't written anything substantial since school, you can always get others to write for you. You can create the outline, then you get a ghostwriter to write the book, report or course.

You can find a ton of people willing to do this for a reasonable price on either Upworthy or Fiverr. Plus, there are many ghostwriting companies on the internet you can use.

OR, take the bull by the horns and do it yourself. Remember, this book is all about doing.

Let's take a look at Amazon.

In 1994, When Jeff Bezos started Amazon. He started an online Bookshop from a run-down old office. Even the Amazon sign in that office was just a large handwritten sign with the word "Amazon" drawn on it.

Bezos quit his job and started an online book business. He had an idea in his head and had a clear vision. His vision was to create the biggest and best online bookshop ever.

People thought Jeff Bezos was a crazy person, they thought no one would ever buy books online. After all, all they had to do was walk into a Barnes and Noble, right?.

WRONG.

He had the vision, long before it became reality. This is how all great people think. They see the idea in action long before it becomes a reality.

His solution was not found just in the books he sold, his solution was, he was catering to people's problems. Firstly the books solved problems, then secondly by delivering to the door solved another problem, as a lot of people are either busy or inherently lazy.

PLUS, everyone loves a parcel delivered to the door, don't they?

The rest, as they say is history, Jeff Bezos, at the time of writing this, is now the richest man in the World. If he can make Billions of dollars by delivering books, and just about everything else you can think of, including the kitchen sink, couldn't you do something big?

What problems could you solve for people?. What problems do you have?. You can have anything in this life except a life free of problems.

You can even use the free resources online to go figure out the answer?. Create a short Report, an eBook or even a book together outlining the strategy on how to solve the exact problem, then sell it online.

Self-publishing online is very much a hot topic right now. Colleagues of mine are making fortunes doing this very thing, there are many, many courses available online on how to do this.

There are also countless videos on YouTube showing you how to do it for free.

It's not unknown for people to make $10,000 - $20,000 dollars a month, or more in the self-publishing business. I know one guy who once made $92,000 in one month doing this.

Our problems are Universal, everyone has them.

So, why don't all people just figure this out for themselves and solve their own problems?.

That's a good question.

The problem is, people tend to be super busy these days and don't have time to trawl the Internet for hours trying to find all the answers. They would much rather you do all the work for them, then put it in an easy to read report and sell it to them.

The more confidential and embarrassing the problem, the more likely a person is to try and solve it online by either buying a book or even buying the cream or pills they need.

Back in 2004, I made a lot of money selling diet pills on eBay for nearly four years. Many people just didn't want to go on a diet or go to the gym, so a pill was convenient for them.

There are hundreds of ailments, where people seek help from a non medical source. This is just the nature of the beast. People want a quick answer to their problems.

Human beings all have annoying problems. We all have parts of us that we just don't like. As our parts wear out, we are far more likely to look for answers to our problems.

When you help people overcome their problems, you add value to their lives. This is your goal. People who consistently add value to others are usually paid very well.

You become the go-to person for that particular problem.

You become the online health coach or the go-to business person who maybe specialises in affiliate marketing or even selling products on eBay or Amazon.

Many people are unaware of what the purpose of actually building a business should be. They tend to focus on just selling a product and making money, in the hope that it all goes well and lasts.

This is a very short term way of thinking. I have explained in an earlier chapter just how quickly a business can fold if you don't give people the value they deserve.

The idea of any business should be to build an army of LOYAL customers, people who are willing to be buyers, over and over again. The longer people stick by you, the better relationship you will build with them, and the more they trust you. The way, they are more likely to buy even more products from you in the future.

I have colleagues in the publishing business who have fans that buy every book they create. This is exactly what you want, loyal fans.

It's like building a fan club, people get to love you and your products and then come back time and time again to buy from you. If you look after them, they will tell others, and do a lot of your marketing for you.

In other words, buying from you should not just be a "one off" experience, you should be out there in the trenches supplying solutions to people on an ongoing basis.

Solve problems for people 24 hours a day. The Internet is a big place. You have access to people in over 200 countries.

Your products can be shown around this global marketplace 24 hours a day on websites like eBay, Etsy, Amazon etc.

Get people to join your mailing list and ask them what other problems they have. Then sell them the solutions.

This way, your customers are helping you to expand your business.

There are around 8 Billion people in the world at the moment and it's growing every day. Over 3 Billion of these people, at the time of writing this are on the Internet. At some stage, most of the world will be online. That's a lot of people that you will be able to reach every day.

Don't just be a business that buys and sells. Inject some heart into your business. Show people that you care, design solutions for them, solve their problems and they will love you for it.

When your customers really love you, money always follows. And this is definitely one business that you can scale and scale your income – to the stars and beyond.

10

FAMILY, FRIENDS AND FOES

I know what you're thinking. What does family & friends have to do with success?. I have to say, it can have everything to do with it.

I'm sure most of us love our families, right?, but isn't it always the way that in order for us to change, we sometimes end up alienating those who are near and dear to us?.

I think most of us have family members that we would do just about anything for. But, as life moves on, so do we, and some of those feelings we have towards certain family members and friends, can change.

And their feelings can change toward us.

Sometimes your friends can become your new family. I know this sounds crazy but sometimes you just connect better with friends who really "get you", as opposed to family, who sometimes don't.

Your family have known you longer than anyone else. They have this set idea about you. They also may have set ideas for you. Of course, not all families try to reign you in to their way of thinking, some family members actually can be very encouraging.

My parents never interfered with my job or business choices, I was lucky, but not all family members can be as encouraging as that.

Because of my insane positive outlook on life I've often been accused of seeing things through rose tinted glasses. The truth is, I just refuse to subscribe to the negativity that some people seem to think is necessary.

There are people out there who reject all forms of positivity. They actually see positive people as a threat to their ideals. They view positive people as Woo Woo Weirdo's.

Trust me, being positive isn't weird.

A positive outlook can only help you and others, it's healthy and most people prefer to see it, after all, many people in this world default to their cynical, negative side.

I call this the dark side.

What good does being negative do?

In my view, you should surround yourself with people who assist you, not those who resist you.

You can end up spending more time with friends than you do with family members, and you can sometimes enjoy being with friends a whole lot more. You sort of adopt really good friends as part of your own family.

Close family members can start to worry about you when you are seemingly changing before their very eyes. As most people live each day as a repeat of the previous day, anyone in the family fold trying to break out of this monotony and trying to be different can often ring alarm bells.

This is quite normal, but nonetheless, it doesn't help you.

When you are trying to push forward, those closest to you can be a hindrance by trying to pull you back into their way of thinking.

There is a common belief out there that "family is everything", and to an extent this is right, many people subscribe to this way of thinking. However, this does not make them right.

The truth is family members often see your life from their own perspective and point of view. They are not always the best people to advise you on your future.

Because family members are "close" this negative vibe can be pretty devastating.

People tend to listen to family as if they are some kind of authority on everything, personally I think this is flawed thinking. My family are great, but none of them are experts on anything i'm involved in, or interested in.

It's a bit like asking a butcher for financial advice, your family are your family, not experts in what is best for you. It's best to keep family at a distance if you can, in the early days of your transformation.

You can be married to someone for years and after time realise that maybe they were not the right person for you after all. This is probably why the divorce rate is so high.

We are born to grow and serve. Everything in nature grows and serves. To stand still is to go against nature.

According to the Office of National Statistics, the divorce rate here in the UK at the time of writing is 42% and is 50% in the USA. Nearly one in 2 marriages end in divorce.

Obviously you can't divorce your Mum and Dad but you don't have to hang on every word they say.

When you got married, perhaps things were perfect. But now, maybe you are going in a totally different direction and are staying together for the sake of the children, or because it seems like it's just too much trouble to split up.

Sometimes it takes very little to fall out with a family member. I remember my mum falling out with my older sister over a remark she made about a photograph, they never spoke again. my point is, it's easy to fall out with family over almost nothing at all.

Many families are dysfunctional, life is much faster now and it may be a sign of the times, but nonetheless, it is what it is.

If you're moving in a different direction to that of your family, keep it under your hat for a while, at least until you've almost achieved your goal, then drop the bomb slowly.

My dad left my mum when I was 13, they just didn't get on. Both of my parents survived the split. My dad went on to run his own business at 65 years of age.

It's not the end of the world if family doesn't see eye to eye anymore.

Not every spouse is supportive. This hurts, as we naturally assume that the person we choose to spend our life with, is going to support us through thick and thin.

That old "for better or worse" doesn't always work if you're struggling to pay the rent and all you want to do is leave your job and start a business.

This of course is not always the case. However, you should always weigh up the pros and cons of any relationship before making any final decision.

Just because your spouse doesn't agree with you doesn't mean you should split up, try to get them on board with your latest venture and sell them on all the benefits of having more money and freedom.

You are not going to be a carbon copy of everyone near and dear to you, it takes courage to break out and be your own person. Celebrate your quirky uniqueness and just go out and do it.

If people really want to make you happy, they will encourage you to achieve what you want in life, even if your ideals are not the same as theirs.

It's ridiculous to think that because you are a family member that you can't think differently from the rest of the family.

I mean, It's not like you belong to the Mafia.

By not supporting you, they are often only trying to make sense of your change, people see things how THEY want to see them, they won't always see things from your perspective.

Sometimes, family are trying to protect you. They don't want you to go out and make a fool of yourself.

Again, I'm not saying ditch your family. Just spend more time with people who are more like you, and who see things from your perspective. Speak to your family and try to find out why they are being unsupportive, it could be something you can both work on.

This may sound harsh but I speak from experience.

I have always been a natural entrepreneur, ever since I was a child, however, none of my family have really been cut from the same tree.

My mum, dad and sisters have always worked, my dad became an entrepreneur later on in life, age 65, however most of my immediate family are not entrepreneurial types.

I don't have a problem with that.

But sometimes it is your family that has a problem with you.

My advice here is to remember that time is very valuable and you don't want to spend your life arguing with your family. Make your mind up to do it anyway.

Please remember:

Success is the best form of revenge. When you are an outstanding success, people will be drawn to you like a magnet.

Until then, keep quiet about your plans. People can't judge you if they don't know what you're doing. I don't know about you but when I have a brilliant idea, I lose a little bit of the enthusiasm for it if I tell someone.

Most people tell you not to bottle things up, but if it's something exciting, don't risk getting a negative blowback from someone, maybe a friend or a family member, which can curb your enthusiasm.

Keep it to yourself until you achieve it, people will soon see the change in you, you won't have to tell them.

That brings another chapter to a close. Now it's time to move on to the "Art of Making Money"

11
THE ART OF MAKING MONEY

Earlier we spoke about the Art of making money and how it is a science, but not an exact science. In this chapter, I'm going to expand on that.

Most books teach you that anyone can make money. I beg to differ. Sure, anyone can make a wage, that's fairly easy, just get a job.

But REAL money?, that's an art.

The Art of making money is like art itself, it's beautiful. We look at it with wonder in our eyes and as we step back away from it, we bask in all its glory.

Making money is an art. It's hours and hours of careful deliberation followed by the master stroke of the brush on the canvas, or as we entrepreneurs call it, "the plan". It takes time and it's not something to be rushed.

Personally, I don't go in for all this get rich quick stuff as even if it does makes money today, it will probably cost me money tomorrow.

If you ever want to see the get rich quick brigade in action just go on to Facebook and you will see many plans and schemes in action. People tend to try many, many schemes before losing all of their fingers.

The Art of making money is to create a long-lasting foundation on which you can build a long-lasting stream of income, then, once you are successful at that, you produce other streams of related income.

In other words, build your business on solid ground, not hearsay or gambling. Although all business can be classed as a bit of a gamble, the art of business is to take measured risks, not reckless risks.

Making large sums of money has almost become this magical thing. A person with money is often admired and looked up to, as if he or she is some kind of celebrity.

The reality is, money is out there in the world for anyone, but very few create what it takes to get it in any large quantity.

It's really all about creating self-belief and developing the confidence you need to create wealth.

This book has all the wisdom you will ever need to create everything you want, but the reader has to implement that knowledge. Let me give you a confidence booster, just in case you need it.

Do you remember something that you were really good at? It may have been something you did at school or something wonderful in adult life.

Can you remember that feeling?

It's like an adrenalin rush. This is the feeling of WINNING. If you could bottle it and sell it, you would make a million.

It's a feeling of "I can do anything", "I can be anything", "I will do it".

This is the confidence you build when you are firing on all six cylinders. This is the feeling of being UNSTOPPABLE.

Do you know what else can produce this amazing burst of confidence?. Answer, making a lot of money. I know this because every time I increase my income by a large amount, I experience these same winning feelings.

My confidence grows each and every time. Money increases confidence, and with that confidence, you will create more money.

That magic buzz of SUCCESS is better than any stimulant you could ever take, and many, many times more powerful.

Our brain send a magnificent high throughout our body when we achieve something very good. It's like those wonderful feelings we experience when we see something of great beauty.

Follow these steps to Victory.

Step up and be bold. Attack, attack, attack. No one got rich by going unnoticed in this World. Get your face out there. Get your name out there. People buy people.

Be BOLD!

Always think you can do something, even if your trembling heart is telling you, maybe you can't. If someone has already done it, you can do it. Don't let yourself down by standing in the way of your own success.

Success comes from multiple failures. People afraid of failure are shooting themselves in the foot. You can't win without experiencing failure. No one hits the bullseye at the first time of asking,

Giving up over and over only makes you good at giving up. You can't be successful by being a professional quitter. Dive deeper, stay longer, adjust your strategy if necessary, but never, never quit.

Next up. We are going to be dealing with one of the biggest problems you will have to deal with when becoming an entrepreneur. **SELF-DOUBT.**

❧ 12 ❧
SELF-DOUBT - WINNING THROUGH IT

All of us at some stage have had some form of nagging self doubt. It's that little voice in the back of our head that tells us that we aren't good enough.

Maybe it was the girl or guy that we should have asked out many years ago, or maybe it was the job that we should have gone for, but didn't.. The point is, something held us back, something prevented us from making that move.

Why do we doubt ourselves?

It could be for many reasons. It could be that we still believe people from our past, who have told us that we were useless, or stupid, sometimes even family members or teachers can utter these words in haste. They can have a profound effect on us, for years afterwards.

Words are very powerful.

It could even be that we judge our self worth by our net worth. Some people don't feel worthy without money. This is a serious mistake.

We are and always will be valuable with or without money. You don't need money to be worthy.

Comparing ourselves to others can also cause self doubt, comparisons are futile, we should like and love ourselves for who WE are.

The journey to a person's success can often involve years of struggle. With my own story of online marketing, I took several years to make a full-time income, yet from day one I was comparing my lack of success with the success of other people, who had probably been doing online marketing for years.

This may seem ridiculous now, but I think that we all engage in this practice of self-doubt at some stage or other.

When we were back in school, we were all bunched together in classrooms, and we were exposed to all kinds of people, some gifted, some not so.

School can be exceptionally cruel at times, as often or not we encounter people with all kinds of genetic advantages that we ourselves don't have.

This could be people with better looks, more talent, etc. These people are often the most popular ones in school. People gravitated towards them.

School can turn into a popularity contest.

If you were not that popular in school, join the club. most people weren't.

Most people are NOT born with genetic advantages. The problem is Society is that TV, the beauty, and the Movie world shows us how, according to them, we should look.

Television itself is full of commercials telling us all what we are missing out on, and what we need to buy to fix it.

The truth is. We are all OK as we are. We don't need fixing. All we need to do if we want to improve our lives is to learn how to grow and serve.

Self doubt is like us putting on the brakes. It stops us from moving forward. We tend to see ourselves as not good enough, even when there is proof to the contrary.

Humans have always doubted themselves, even millionaires doubt themselves sometimes.

In order to grow and serve, we need to change our habits. Self-doubt is really just an ingrained thought and feeling that becomes a habit.

What can we replace it with?.

I'm glad you asked that. Confidence. Ah, yes, good old confidence.

How do you get confident?.

You take a step over the ledge. You step forward and do the very things that you are afraid of. Remember, the things you fear, are probably the very things that you should be doing. Self-confidence comes from over-riding that fear and doing the very things you are afraid of.

Self-doubt starts to fade once you see your results.

When I started my first online business back in 2010, I was full of self-doubt. I thought to myself. "Who am I to try to teach people things, I don't even know what i'm doing myself".

Imagine if I had listened to myself?. I certainly wouldn't have written this book. That doubting voice within is trying to sabotage us. Don't listen to it.

The more we doubt ourselves, the more we build the habit of doubting ourselves. The more we have confidence in ourselves, the more we build the habit of confidence.

Self-doubt encourages the habit of putting things off. Confidence encourages the habit of getting things done.

Flip that switch in your head.

Self doubt is only a thought, or series of thoughts. Are you going to be ruled by a thought?

What proof have you to doubt, yourself?. Have you tried and failed?. did you try EVERYTHING?.

What about all the things that you've done right in the past?, did you question those too?.

The hardest thing we do will always be taking the first step. The motivation to take the second step comes from making that first step.

Once you take your foot off the brake and make that first step. It will feel good. Oh, so good.

There is never going to be a perfect time to do anything, you only have now, this moment.

Doubting yourself leads to nothing, or at least, very little being done. We gain confidence by doing.

Self doubt will slowly disappear when you start to create forward momentum. You can only get that momentum by taking your foot off the brake.

Celebrate each and every success you have, no matter how small it is. Reward yourself for each successful step.

Don't Be Like Them.

Life is full of watchers, people who watch other people become successful and wish it was them. But action takers, the real doers of the world, these people are not quite so common.

Everything you eat, read, watch & wear, even the places you work in, all were created by doers. Doers move the World. Without doers, the World would be a desert, a no man's land.

All of those doers had to overcome self-doubt. Self-doubt exists in us all, but many overcome it and go on to move mountains.

You can too. Just release the brake.

None of us has an unlimited amount of life left in front of us. We don't know when our time will come to exit, but come it will. We can either make the rest of our lives the best of our lives or we can live it by regretting the things that we didn't push ourselves to do.

This chapter is a bit of a wake-up call. Every day we have the same 24 hours in our day as everyone else.

It's far better to try and fail, than to not try at all. If you try and fail, you will hopefully learn the lesson. If you never try, you will spend your life wondering what might have been.

Trying and failing builds resilience. It builds power.

It doesn't make sense to spend your life putting things off. Self-doubt keeps us small. It keeps us from living life to the fullest. We are all a lot more than we show and know, we become more by doing more.

Some people spend their entire lives on hold. Each week, month or year is just a carbon copy of the last. Instead of living 70 years, they live one year, 70 times.

We are curious creatures with a powerful brain. We are not designed to be silent. Our hearts and minds are designed to express ourselves, and follow our dreams.

I don't believe we were put on this earth to just reproduce, pay bills and die. There is more to life than that.

We should be maxing out our happiness.

We should be increasing our potential.

We should be striving for the best.

We all matter.

Take that first step today, not tomorrow, or next week. Do something today that will move your life forward.

Create your own momentum, don't always be looking for motivation from others, motivate yourself.

Remember, motivation comes from doing.

Let go of that self-doubt from within yourself, build the confidence that you need to get your foot off the brake.

Life is more fun when you let go, and be your true self.

Think of how much better your life will be, once you get the results you want.

See you in the next chapter..

13

THE ENEMY WITHIN

Life really is this huge mixture of things that we love to do, mixed with things that we're not very keen on doing, topped off with several obstacles that we have to overcome.

Problems often appear out of nowhere, and just when things are running along smoothly, BOOM! here comes another problem.

This is not good luck or bad luck, this is life. Our lives are about facing problems and overcoming them the best we can.

There is though, one big, giant problem that many people have a constant problem with, yes, you guessed it. It's us.

More often than not, we are our very own worst enemy. If only we could get out of our own way, life would be much more simple.

Human beings tend often overcomplicate the simplest of things, I see this all the time in business, and getting out of our own way can be very difficult. After all, we have a lifetime of habitual thoughts swishing around in our heads, that we, ourselves created.

When we are younger, we tend to exist a lot on our ego system. We thought, back then that we knew even more than our parents.

When we get to our mid twenties, our view of the world starts to change, and we start to realize that not everything evolves around us.

If we are humble enough to accept this, by now we might even admit that we were wrong.

I know, it is sometimes hard to admit it when you're wrong. I struggled with this for a long time, I felt like every time I admitted I was wrong, I was admitting that I was a failure. This of course isn't true. Every time you're wrong, it's a lesson.

Hopefully, we learn from the lessons that life gives us, and boy, do they give us some lessons to learn.

We often treat people badly, then feel guilty afterwards, sometimes for years. We often don't think about the effect our words and actions have on other people. When the ego rules, we are not always a nice person to be around.

In fact, most of us are guilty of behaving badly at some time or another. We wouldn't be human if we lived our lives like saints.

At some stage we really need to let go of thinking we are right all the time and realise that in order to move on we have to get out of our own way, and listen to the wisdom of others.

Moving on is the best thing we can do. Let it go and move on. Stop living in the past.

We can choose to just survive, or we can choose to thrive. The real truth is, we are all the engineers of our own life. No one else is involved. We design our own lives.

We always have a choice.

All of our thoughts, habits and actions have brought us to this point in our lives.

It lies with us now, how we are going to proceed from this point on.

Do we just carry on doing the same things over and over again, expecting different results, or do we change our habits from this day on?

Again, it's a choice.

Where will you be in a year's time? what about 5 years' time. Think about it. If you don't know where you'll be in five years' time, you're probably already there.

Do you have friends?, I'm sure you do. Do they work?, do they complain about their work?

This is how a lot of people live their lives. They complain about everything, but do nothing to change.

If you work in McDonald's, but you want to be a Chef du Cuisine, you're going to have to move up the ladder. Learn more skills. It's the same as if you earn a few hundred dollars a week, and you want to be a millionaire, you have to move up the ladder.

In order to be successful, you have to think and feel like you already are successful. In order to attract success, you have to get rid of those old thought patterns that are holding you back.

It's not wrong to want more. We all deserve to get the best out of our lives. As Michael Douglas said in the 1987 Wall Street film, "There is no nobility in poverty".

You are not doing anyone any service at all by being broke. Least of all, yourself.

My point here is, you can spend the next few years doing the same old thing and get the same old results or you can change today, get out of your own way and rewrite the script.

You are the star of your own movie. How that movie works out is up to you. The script is in your hands right now. Will it be a movie worth paying to see?

Instead of focusing on your problems, focus on other people's problems, and monetise them, this is how you become rich. What can you provide that solves the problems that other people have.

Master this and the money will follow.

If you want to attract good things in your life, have faith in the future. Get out of your own way, and let the fun begin.

See you in the next chapter.

14

NICHES AND RICHES

Fortune favours the brave.

Pick a niche that resonates with you. A niche that you feel you can build a business around. One you can stick at. Let's say you live a healthy lifestyle and you love working out.

So you choose the Health & Beauty niche. Health and Beauty in itself is very popular, but also it's ultra competitive. My advice here is to niche down, find a section of health and beauty that is profitable enough to make money from, but is not overrun with competitors.

If you think of health & beauty as the Pie. The sub-niche, or micro-niche, is your slice of the pie. When you make a success of it, that's the cherry on top.

What a lot of people do when they go into business is they do everything and try to cater for everyone. This is a big mistake as you end up catering for no one.

You can't treat a business like a Chinese buffet, picking at everything. Stick with one niche, and niche down to find a sub-niche that works well for you.

If you look at any successful business, it tends to focus on one thing, and will try to dominate one niche. Steve jobs dominated and created those weird, but nice-looking Apple (c) desktop computers before they added other electronic products, such as the iPod and iPhone.

Steve Jobs focused on one idea first, then later on added other related ideas to his business. This produced a billion dollar business over time.

They didn't try to sell shoes as well. They stuck with one idea and made it work.

How do we know if the niche is profitable?, That's simple, are there enough people in the niche who buy enough products to support a business in that niche?.

You need tenacity, hard work, and laser focus to succeed. You must live it and breathe it, until it becomes your reality.

When I built my first business, I gave up most of my leisure time, I let go of holidays and weekends away for a while. If your partner is a bit reluctant, you will need to bring them into line with your vision and sell them on the idea of the better lifestyle you expect to create for both of you.

Better still, bring them on board, make them a part of the business.

So, what does being Rich really mean to you?

For some people, they would feel Rich if they had another few thousand a year. To others, they wouldn't think they were rich unless they had a $1,000,000 a year.

Ultimately, $1,000,000 does not go very far these days. After taxes etc, you wouldn't be left with a great deal out of that million. Nowadays, you are more likely to want or need at least $10,000,000 to call yourself Rich.

So how can you obtain $10,000,000?

Does this seem impossible? well, let's chunk that figure down.

If you created a digital course and sold it for $1000 profit, you would need to sell 1,000 of them to reach $1,000,000. Do this for 10 years and you'll get that $10,000,000

If you created a course that sold for $2000 profit, you would need to sell 5000. If you sold a thousand courses a year, it would take just 5 years to reach $10,000,000

If you started a membership site charging $27 a month, you would need just over 3086 members to bring you in around $1,000,000 a year. In 10yrs, you would have reached your $10,000,000 goal.

Nothing is beyond the realms of possibility. Making money is an art form, as I said earlier, so in order to create that art, you need to create a formula that works for you.

I've given you every possible angle to make money in this book. You now need to create a plan.

Step 1. Work out what type of business suits you?

Step 2. What niche or micro niche do you think you could dominate?

Step 3. How could you best serve that niche?. An online business or a brick and mortar business?

Step 4. How much time will you put by each day to work on that business?

Step 5. Set business and financial goals for the first 3 months, 6 months 1yr, 2, 3 etc

Step 6. Create a plan to attain this goal.

Step 7. START.

At first, it might seem impossible, maybe you are short of money.

If you are short of money, do what I did to start my first business online, create an eBay business or a print on demand business printing T shirts, mugs etc. SELL something. You will find a way.

Once you start to make some real money, you can compound it by putting it back into the business and growing your business, You do this by increasing your advertising budget etc.

Let's say you start off in the Real Estate business and you start with a loan. You buy and sell your first property and make a profit. You then invest that profit into another property, and then flip that one.

You keep rolling this money over and over, until you start to accumulate several properties. Maybe when you started you were flipping lower price properties, after you have rolled over the profits a few times, you could now be flipping higher price properties..

It's better than flipping burgers.

According to Credit Suisse's new Global Wealth Report 2017, there are now 36,000,000 millionaires in the World. That's 36 Million, Millionaires in the World today.

Think about that. There are only 7.53 Billion people on the planet (2017)

It really isn't that hard to be a millionaire these days. Especially now that we have the Internet.

You have access to a global audience. You don't have to spend fortunes on newspaper and TV advertising anymore to get customers.

We now have social media. We now have Pay Per Click advertising. You can get eyeballs to your offers for a very low cost.

People are starting businesses online for a few hundred dollars. Gone are the days when you needed tens of thousands of dollars to get started.

Here are some ideas to get you started:

Affiliate Marketing. This is where you sell other people's products on commission. Orders are fulfilled by the product creator. No stock or outlay (apart from advertising, is required)

Dropshipping. This is where you sell products, you mark up the product at one price and the dropshipper sends the item to your customer for a fixed price. The difference between the dropshipper's price and your sale price, is your profit.

There is no upfront stock or outlay, apart from advertising costs. Currently sites like eBay will allow dropshipping, but this could change in the future.

Amazon FBA (Fulfilled by Amazon), this is where you order goods from wholesalers and send them direct to any one of Amazon's global warehouses. You list them on Amazon, and Amazon sort, deliver and also take a cut of the sale price, when sold.

Creating your own Web-store This is where you purchase goods from a wholesaler and sell them in your own store. You keep all the profit and send the goods to the customer. Shopify offer ready-made stores that you can add products to and customise with your logo, and brand colours. You will need some capital for products, advertising and store costs.

Membership Sites Do you have a passion or hobby that others would readily pay you to learn?. There are hundreds of thousands of subjects that can be monetised in this way. There are tons of membership sites out there online charging monthly or fixed fees. If you are good at creating content, why not go for this option?

Selling a Service Do you have a marketable skill?. Can you do Search Engine Optimisation?, can you write articles?. Can you design websites or webpages?, or are you good at graphic design?. If you can, sell these services to others, online.

Outsourcing a Service. There are people doing this online all the time. They advertise web services, and then get someone else to do them. Let's say you advertise that you can create websites. You charge one price and get the job outsourced at a lower price.

The difference between what you charge and what you pay the outsourcer, is your profit.

Network Marketing This made me a lot of money a few years ago, It's a way of being in business, but you're not in business alone. You build a team of similar business people like yourself who also go out and build their own teams.

You get a cut of the profit from their sales as well as your own. Many people have created 6 and 7 figure incomes from network marketing. It's a great, low-cost way of getting into business, with minimal overheads.

Selling on eBay This is one of my favourites. I did this full-time between 2004 and 2008. First, sell any stuff in your house that you no longer need, then use that cash to buy stock.

I sold my entire personal development book collection on there for £250 (approx $320), and bought two crates of diet pills from the USA. I turned that into an £800 ($1030) per week business for nearly 4 yers. I was also a Gold Powerseller on eBay. All from just £250 start up capital.

Creating your own digital products. People all over the world have problems. You can capitalise on their problems by helping to solve them, whether it's acne or lack of Money, create digital reports (eBooks, etc) and then sell them online.

Self Publishing. This is probably one of the best online businesses today. You can do this even if you can't write your own books. Publish paperbacks, Kindle Books and Audios on Amazon & Audible. You can use a ghostwriter if you are not confident in writing your own books.

Print on Demand. This where you can sell mugs, T Shirts and other accessories with printed logos, funny quotes and all kinds of other crazy stuff on them. This is a fun business that you can start with very little money.

You can sell the items on Etsy & eBay, you take the orders and the fulfilment company will print them and deliver them to your customer.

I think this gives you a few ideas to get started. All of these ideas can be profitable, if you put the work in.

I've also done Blogging. This works well if you can create good content and drive plenty of traffic to it . This is the key to success online, getting people to actually see your offers.

Of course, with Amazon, eBay & Etsy, you can leverage off of their own traffic, which is ideal if you haven't yet learned to get traffic.

I truly believe that there has never been a better time than right now to make money. We live in a digital age, nearly everyone has a smartphone and a computer. It has never been a better time in history, to sell to a global audience.

This book has covered exactly how to develop the mindset to create riches. Bear in mind that riches are not just money. You also need good health to enjoy life, and good people to enjoy it with, never neglect your health or your friends and family, for the sake of Money.

You can always make more money, but some things, like relationships, are irreplaceable.

Money is there to enjoy and to be shared. It gives you the ability to help other people, and that will increase your happiness and satisfaction levels.

As with all things in life, there are no guarantees, but it's very hard to stop a person from succeeding if they are really determined to do it.. It's all about how bad you really want to succeed.

You can't expect to get anything with a half-hearted effort, unfortunately a lot of people who start out with good intentions to start a business, give up halfway through or just a few feet from the finish line. A few more steps and they would have been successful.

Master one thing at a time. Steer yourself away from comfortable times and get those palms sweating. That is the feeling of excitement, the excitement you get when you know you're going to WIN.

GO ALL IN.

It has to be a deep desire. The desire to attain this goal is what keeps you going when things are not working out. Tough times don't last but tough people do, a lot of people are tough on the surface but very few are mentally tough too.

Being truly focused and obsessed on one thing and making that one thing work will end up getting you the results you want.

I have never met anyone in business who wasn't obsessed with the end result. I've met a few wannabe's but none of those people made it work.

Could you imagine someone who wants to be a top footballer being only just a little bit interested in being a top footballer?. No, neither can I. It's the same with starting a business and becoming rich. You have to make it a healthy obsession.

Success is a partnership between you, and your subconscious mind. You create this business of yours in the mind, put it down on paper, and then act it out in reality.

Remember, you are building something here which eventually will give you the financial resources to create a life of freedom for you and your loved ones.

Freedom is never free, there is always a cost, most people are too attached to working the 40 to 50 hour work week for 40 to 50 years to ever get off the treadmill to nowhere.

YOU HAVE TO GET OFF

I say this not to make you feel bad, but to make you feel good about changing. I have been on that treadmill many times in between starting a business, and it's not a very nice treadmill to be on.

I know there are a million and one distractions going on in your life right now. I know you have reasons to NOT get started, the time is never right, the money is too low, the kids are screaming all the time, but you have to let go and put your trust in you.

You have to make the time, you have to find the time, you have to work around your job, the kids etc. This is what entrepreneurs do.

Be resourceful.

If you want your business to prosper, think of it as a plant, and grow it every day. Give it your 100% attention, look after it and eventually, it will look after you.

Here are some home truths about getting rich from my own personal experience.

On the journey toward riches, successful people often tend to live below their means. This is not because they are broke, but because they use their cash to buy assets for the business.

I have seen many a budding businessperson run out of money simply because they gave themselves the title of CEO then started behaving like John D. Rockefeller.

Don't live beyond your means, live below them.

ACT YOUR WAGE...

Instead of spending big money on TV's and Cars, entrepreneurs tend to spend money on their business, after all, this is your future we're talking about here.

Have you ever noticed how many "broke" people always find money for big TV's, booze, cigarettes, and expensive trainers etc?

When spending money. Ask yourself "do I really need this?" or is it just something I want, to make me feel good for now?

Broke people also tend to spend more than they earn, having ongoing balances outstanding on Credit cards. This is more like a live now and pay later kind of attitude.

This is why the Lottery is so popular, it gives people hope even though the odds are so outrageously low of hitting the Jackpot. The lottery provides funds for good causes, however yours isn't usually one of them.

If you're going to be Rich, you really need to delay gratification until you have so much money that you can actually afford luxuries without using credit cards.

Even then, rich people remain rich by living below their actual incomes.

If you earn a £1,000,000 a year but spend £250,000, you'll always have money. If you earn a £1,000,000 a year and spend £1,000,000 or more, you'll be broke if the money stops coming in.

Millionaires do dress smartly at times, however they are often seen wearing casual clothes and driving mediocre vehicles. Check out Mark Zuckerberg of Facebook fame, he's a billionaire, yet he wears the same style of casual clothing (and colour) every day, usually a black T shirt and jeans. He also drives a VW Golf (as of the time of writing this book)

Anyone can look rich. The trick is to be rich and not always look it.

Obviously, there are exceptions out there. some people love to flaunt their wealth, such as people who own yachts, race horses and Ferraris. However, these people tend to be super-rich and not just the basic millionaires who only own a mere million or two.

Don't consider yourself rich until you have at least $10,000,000.

As I've mentioned earlier. A million dollars (or pounds) won't get you very far these days. In fact, in many areas of the UK and America, it won't even get you a decent house.

You'll need more than a million to be rich.

See you at the Bank...

15

UNCLUTTER YOUR LIFE

We seem to live in a World where collecting as much stuff as possible is quite the norm. You often walk by a house where the garage is stuffed to the rafters with yes, you guessed it, more stuff.

It's almost like a "badge of honour" to cram as much stuff as possible into our houses. Most of which is just collecting dust.

Some people leave the car on the driveway because there is so much stuff in the garage.

As consumers, we feel it is our duty to buy stuff. You see people going bananas at Christmas buying more and more stuff. At the drop of a hat we seem to look for any excuse to spend money and buy even more stuff.

The ad companies spend millions convincing us how our lives are much worse off if we don't buy their stuff.

Here's a novelty. Learn to let go of the impulse to collect stuff.

I know it's cool to always have the latest iPhone etc, but what happened to all the old iPhones, did you junk them, recycle them, or are they gathering dust in your house?.

I know from personal experience, I have at least four old phones hanging around the house.

In business, you have to learn to let go of money. Keeping a hold on money for dear life is not a sign of an abundant mindset, in fact, it's the opposite.

In business, sometimes you win and sometimes you lose. Not all the money that you invest in a business will work out well for you.

The problem a lot of people have is letting go of any money. They want to start a business for free, but they also want customers to pay for their stuff.

It's not going to happen.

Learning to let go of money, starts with learning to let go of stuff. This really is a case of less is more. I've often heard people on the Internet baulk at spending a few hundred dollars to start a business, yet, they are quite happy to have thousands of dollars worth of stuff sitting in the loft or the garage doing absolutely nothing.

It doesn't make a lot of sense. If you need money to start a business, sell some of your stuff.

We need to get our heads around buying all this stuff and collecting it. It's time that we all realise, if you are trying to build a better life and are looking for seed capital to do so, all this buying of stuff is really keeping you poor.

When we can let go, sell, or give away our stuff, we are simply recycling it back to a source that needs or wants it more than us.

Letting go can give us a huge sense of freedom and just giving or selling our old stuff can be the first stage of learning to let go.

I sold my house in 2017, I had plenty of stuff, I wasn't immediately going to buy another house, so I had a dilemma. Store it, sell it, or give it away.

I chose to give it all away to charity. Do you know how freeing that was?. I felt good, plus I felt uncluttered.

I put what little stuff I had left, computer etc into the boot of my car and drove off into the sunset.

For the next few months I toured the UK, my only belongings were those that I could fit in my car.

I actually spent months on the road, stopping off at a different hotel or B&B each night. Not having to drag all my old junk around with me was a very freeing experience.

Let's be honest, all we really need is food, a car, a roof over our heads, clothes a phone and a laptop. Perhaps a TV if you're into that, but that's really all we need.

Letting go of things enables us to free our minds of the need to consume and collect. Once we know that everything is available in abundance, we will attract more money.

Whilst traveling, I leveraged the money I made on the house to create an income. I would literally find a wifi hotspot and work online for an hour or two a day to bring in money. McDonalds was often my office, as the wifi is pretty good there.

Holding on to money teaches our subconscious that money is hard to come by, therefore our actions are always aimed towards hanging on to it.

I'm not talking about being silly with money and throwing it away, I'm talking about investing your money in yourself and your business. Money makes more money, it always has and always will.

Having thousands of dollars worth of stuff lying around in the house doing nothing, is not a good idea if you're looking to expand financially.

Get rid of the old collecting habits, if you must collect something, collect money.

There are many books out there that teach people how to make money. However very few ever talk about this subject of learning to let go.

One of the most pleasurable aspects of having money is to know that if you spend some, there is always more.

You no longer have to hang on to everything you earn or buy. Recycling what you no longer need is much more fun.

Stuff will never make you happy, nor will money but money will solve many problems, and make life a little easier.

We tend to want stuff, then once we have it we want something else.

Stuff, is meant to be recycled. When you no longer wear those clothes, don't keep them in storage for ever and a day, recycle them by either giving them to someone less fortunate or sell them and give that money to someone less fortunate..

What comes around goes around. You recycle goods or money, and goods or money will eventually find its way back to you.

You have to let go in order to receive more.

It's just like the Junk we feed our brains every day. If your headspace gets overrun with stuff, it starts to affect your thinking, we start to think like the junk we collect.

You've probably heard that old saying, garbage in equals garbage out.

A more focused headspace, free from junk and a less cluttered living space, can set each and every one of us free.

Less is more.

I think far too many of us buy stuff just to have stuff around. We spend money trying to impress people who very often we don't really care about anyway, we are just looking to gain the upper hand by trying to impress upon them that we can afford good "stuff" too.

I had a friend who used to know how well I was doing by my car. Or so he thought. The truth was I always bought a car worth less than I could afford. No one ever knew what I could afford, and I preferred it that way.

Let's look at what wealthy people do. Please note, being rich is not the same as being wealthy. True wealth comes from investing in things that increase in value, not from buying things that decrease in value.

Most really wealthy people do not go out and buy brand new cars or live in million dollar mansions. They live below their means and invest in creating residual income streams that keep on going. This way, if one income stream dries up, they have others to fill the gaps.

Real wealthy people tend to buy cars at least 3 years old and live in houses well below the standard that they can actually afford.

Why?. Because they are in it for the long term.

Check out Lottery winners. More than 60% of them go back to where they were before they won after a few short years. They spend, spend, spend, then have to sell it all just to keep going.

Not so for the shrewd person who keeps an eye on the bottom line and uses their money to invest in assets. Remember, if you spend $7 Million on a home, that's $7 Million you can't invest.. And NO, buying a house is not really an investment any more, if you live in it. It's only an investment if you buy a house to rent out or sell for a profit.

So Why Do We Collect Things?

We collect things in our lives for various reasons. It can be simple comfort bingeing, maybe caused by unhappiness or it could even be because we have become habitual consumers.

Buying things (retail therapy) is very pleasurable and can be very addictive. Every time we buy something we get a dopamine hit in our brain, this pleasure chemical is like having a large dose of chocolate, very pleasurable, but, can also be very addictive.

Retail outlets need you to keep buying and buying. They make it very easy for you with their in house credit cards or no interest credit deals.

No one actually needs the latest iPhone, but millions of people buy it and often queue outside the stores for long hours to be one of the first people to get their hands on it.

When you buy a new car, thousands of pounds have been wiped off the value of it as you drive it out of the showroom. But people still love buying new cars.

When we collect junk in our life, we act like junk. We overflow with thoughts of junk and our actions are all about junk.

Junk Media is all around us. Fake news, fake this and fake that. It pierces our brain and penetrates our thoughts every day with misinformation, it also breeds fear. Political dogma is spouted by overpaid people with different agendas every day on our TV's.

Declutter your life, simplify your living and your workspace, tune out from the junk, the gloom and the doom etc. And best of all, stop over-consuming stuff and start BOOMING!..

YES!, use that spare cash to invest in things that increase in value, not things that devalue and drain your cash and your mental reserves.

Onwards and upwards..

16

THE FANTASY OF LUCK

Would I consider myself a lucky person?. I guess I would, however I have had terrible times and tragedy in my life, just like many people.

I guess I just didn't ponder on it.

In the last 2 decades I lost my dad to Cancer, my mum to Alzheimer's and my 31 year old girlfriend to pneumonia. I say this because things happen in life that you have no control over, and if you live long enough you will also see many of those people you love, will depart this world.

I often hear people talk about luck as if it were something that is assigned to them by pure chance, and it is either good or bad. The truth is all of us are on the receiving end of good or bad things.

Luck is not out to get you, it's just there.

We can name these events that happen to us as luck if we choose to. But in reality what happens to us is 5% out of our control, and 95% controlled by us.

So, you could say, 5% of what happens to us could be termed luck.

We can't control everything that happens to us, but we can control most of it. We can also always control how we react to it.

Luck is a very emotive subject, especially if you gamble.

Gamblers swear by it and there are really two sides to luck which I will explain here. The fantasy, and the reality.

The Fantasy

People often describe themselves as either a lucky or unlucky person.

In truth, there are no unlucky or lucky people, there are only people who direct themselves toward favourable or unfavourable circumstances. If you take the short cut home after dark through a deserted car park, the chances are you may get attacked and robbed. If you choose to take the well lit main road, but longer way home, or indeed get a taxi, the chances are you won't.

You don't get on the end of good or bad luck by some mystical force. You get on the end of good luck, simply by working hard, working smart and meeting opportunities head on.

In other words, motion in the right direction will put you in the path of opportunity.

You get on the end of bad luck (most of the time) by thinking bad things are going to happen to you, and always thinking you are going to screw things up.

By having a negative attitude, you attract people and situations in sync with your continuous bad thoughts.

The Reality

Apart from the 5% of things that happen to us which is out of our control, you create your own luck. It's not a magical force that the Gods thrust upon you, or something you buy in a bottle.

We create good or bad luck by our attitude, our choices and our decisions, it's as simple as that.

How does this affect us making money?

Making money is an attitude, it's a frame of mind we either adapt or we don't. We will never attract something we think is impossible to achieve. We will never attract something, while we concentrate on the lack of it.

The true art of making money is to first believe in yourself. Next you have to believe that it is possible. Then you need to take the appropriate actions to get it.

Don't concentrate on whether you are an unlucky or lucky person. You are neither. You can only attract good luck and good fortune by making it happen yourself.

Other people are not specifically put on this earth to help you get rich. You have to take full responsibility for this yourself. Only when you start to make things happen will opportunity come knocking.

The dreaded unpredictable 5%

You can't avoid this. 5% of what happens to us, is totally unpredictable. This 5% is the unknown. It's being in the right or wrong place at the right or wrong time.

You can secure your house like Fort Knox with alarm systems all over the place but one day some sneaky person may find a way in and burgle your house.

You could be perfectly healthy, you may keep fit, watch what you eat, but one day you may have a heart attack.

Who knows?

You can't spend your life expecting or waiting for the worse. You must spend your life expecting the best, and you will finally change your luck.

If I come out of my house, cross the road safely, but a bus mounts the sidewalk and runs me over, that was not something I could have knowingly avoided. This was the unpredictable 5% that I could not avoid.

Yes, I could have walked out of my house 2 minutes later, or earlier and I would have avoided this incident, but I didn't. It felt right to cross the road right now, at this time.

Sometimes your gut feeling can warn you and help you avoid things, and it pays to listen to it, we call it intuition.

But it won't work 100% of the time.

If someone bets black on the Roulette table and puts $40,000 on it and it comes up black, that's luck, even though the odds are evens, that's just good luck. It could just have easily come up red or gone on the green, which goes to the house.

Remember, luck is not out to get you. Don't convince yourself that this is the case or you'll just get a whole lot more bad luck.

Next time something bad happens to you, don't say to yourself "well that's just my luck", that is just asking for trouble, literally.

Always believe that you are going to receive good fortune. Put yourself in front of opportunity, work hard at being a success and treat others how you would like to be treated yourself, with respect, and you'll avoid most of what we call bad luck.

If you truly apply these lessons to your life, you will get better, and your life will get better.

There are no guarantees in life, we are all responsible for ourselves, however each and every one of us can improve our lot.

See yourself for what you really are. A wonderful human being.

If you decide to be, you can be unstoppable. You will gain more confidence, and with that confidence you will achieve more, much more.

And Finally

Everyone has to start somewhere. If you want to achieve Millionaire status you've got to start thinking like a millionaire would think. Look for interviews with millionaires on YouTube and model these people.

View money in the right frame of mind. View it as an unlimited asset that can help a lot of people. Make it, use it, give it, enjoy it. It's there to distribute.

At the end of the road, when your time is up it won't matter how much money you have, what will matter is did you truly live?. Did you achieve all the things you wanted, did you see and experience all the places you wanted to go?

Money is not designed to make you happy. It's designed to give you things to make your life better, to make life easier and to reduce problems, that in itself will make you more happy.

I believe everyone can make a difference, we all come into this world naked like a baby, and we leave the same way. It's what we do in between that really counts. It's not just about making loads of money, it's about being a better person and in turn helping others to be better people too.

My greatest joy in life is to see people succeed. Especially at business. Helping people to be better people, can also make you happy.

I hope you have enjoyed this book, reread it over and over, especially if you're having a down in the dumps day. Down days don't last, learn to dodge the bullets, be nice to yourself and to others.

Can I ask you for a small favour. If you enjoyed this book as much as I have enjoyed writing it, could you leave me a nice review on Amazon?.

Reviews mean a great deal to me. It helps me improve and lets me know what you got out of reading this book.

Reviews help me to get more people to see the book and helps more people to get a copy of it. I would really love to know what you thought of this book.

Thanking you in advance..

I wish you a blessed life.

Keith

References:

Chapter 3 - 1 Financial Times - Plan for five careers in a lifetime - Sept 5 2017

Chapter 3 - 2 The Daily Telegraph - Million would die before they're old enough for Pension - 19 Nov 2005

Chapter 3 - 3 Yahoo Finance - 64% of Americans aren't prepared for retirement - Sept 23 2019

Chapter 9 - 1 Forbes - The 80/20 Rule and how it can change your life - March 7 2016

CONCLUSION

Keep a lookout for new books from me. Follow my Author's page on Amazon to get notifications of new titles from me.

And finally.

There will always be a reason to not do something. There will always be someone telling you, that you can't do something.

Just like you need to ignore the chatter in your head, you also need to ignore negative influences, or better still separate yourself entirely from them.

We all only have so many hours in the day. We can choose to waste them, or use them wisely. What you do now, today will affect your future. Possibly forever.

Remember

Those people you admire, those people doing what you want to do, they all started somewhere. They had big bills to pay, families, debts, lack of funds etc, they had challenges, but they just got on with it.

Once you lead with your heart, your head will follow. The first step leads to the second step and before you know it, all those fears and doubts will slowly disappear.

You can't be great just by thinking great things.

It's better to take action even if you don't have all the facts in place than to sit around waiting for that perfect moment.

As you know, the perfect moment never arrives.

I wish you well in your journey. Let me know what you thought of this book, hopefully it be the first of many.

Don't forget to put everything you've learnt in this book into action.

I would also be very grateful if you could leave me a review on Amazon.

Thank you.

Don't just be great, be AWESOME..

RESOURCES

Come and join me in my private facebook group. It's called Inspired To Make Money and it is full of great ideas to build your perfect side-hustle or full-time business, with a dabble of inspiration.

This could be your daily go-to group for inspiring ways to make money. Join us, it's free.

I have special free gift for you here: https://keitheverett.co.uk/special

Also, why not check out my personal blog for more Inspiration and great money making ideas keitheverett.co.uk

www.ingramcontent.com/pod-product-compliance
Lightning Source LLC
Chambersburg PA
CBHW031545080526
44588CB00018B/2706